Prais

"Terryl's work is incredibly thoughtful. It will appeal to those who view intellectual inquiry as an expression of discipleship. It refrains from demonizing doubt and frames struggle and uncertainty as steppingstones rather than stumbling blocks in the disciple's journey."

—DANIEL BECERRA, Assistant Professor of Church History and Doctrine, Brigham Young University

"Givens engages bright thinkers from women and men, throughout history, and around the globe, to deliver a vision that is life changing. Deeply rooted in the Latter-day Saint gospel to which he is devoted, here are fresh but grounded approaches to discipleship, redemption, and healing. I highly recommend reading this invitation to a more abundant life."

—KATE HOLBROOK, Managing Historian, Church History Department

"This little gem is a guide for the perplexed seeking truth about the highest purpose for life and the best way to live. It cuts to the core of our human dilemma: our most important questions cannot be resolved with certainty, so we are forced to trust our beliefs in order to do anything at all. This entails deciding who is trustworthy, since our beliefs arise in the process of learning from others. Givens is a persuasive guide to texts, people, and ideas that help us make trustworthy, lifelong commitments and remain lifelong truth seekers."

—Charles Randall Paul, author of *Converting the Saints: A Study of Religious Rivalry in America*

"In *Doors of Faith*, Terryl Givens invites us to step into a more expansive experience and understanding of Christ's gospel. It is a plea for us to question preconceptions that may keep doors of faith closed and that get in the way of a more intimate relationship with our divine parents. It is a challenge to put our spiritual imagination to work in opening new doors by actively participating in the unfolding Restoration. It is an invitation to step through doors of faith that open into richer aesthetic, intellectual, and tangible engagement with the world. Finally, it is a challenge to the current generation to rise to one of our age's great opportunities and urgent needs: the re-enchantment of a flat, secular world."

—Bill Turnbull, Co-Founder, Faith Matters Foundation

"Terryl Givens tunes his vast erudition to a personal key in *The Doors of Faith*. Distilling the discoveries of his eminent career studying the Latter-day Saints, he addresses the essential questions that face disciples young and old: Who is God? How shall I believe? Why must mortality buffet its sojourners, and what awaits the wounded? His wager is that a discipleship deeply informed by the rich intellectual beauty of the Christian gospel—what he calls a "witting mind"—is able to treat the spiritual malaise of the moment. Drawing from science, philosophy, history, and literature, he offers an expansive portrait of a Latter-day Saint tradition grounded in early Christian teachings but equal to the challenges of modernity. In the process, he makes a persuasive argument for the indispensable work of theology, always Givens's native tongue."

—Rosalynde Welch, author of *Ether: A Brief Theological Introduction*

THE
DOORS
OF
FAITH

A
Living Faith
Book

Living Faith books are for readers who cherish the life of the mind and the things of the Spirit. Each title offers an example of faith in search of understanding, the unique voice of a practicing scholar who has cultivated a believing heart.

OTHER LIVING FAITH BOOKS INCLUDE:

Adam S. Miller, *Letters to a Young Mormon* (2nd ed.)

Samuel M. Brown, *First Principles and Ordinances: The Fourth Article of Faith in Light of the Temple*

Steven L. Peck, *Evolving Faith: Wanderings of a Mormon Biologist*

Patrick Q. Mason, *Planted: Belief and Belonging in an Age of Doubt*

Ashley Mae Hoiland, *One Hundred Birds Taught Me to Fly: The Art of Seeing God*

Thomas F. Rogers, *Let Your Hearts and Minds Expand: Reflections on Faith, Reason, Charity, and Beauty*

George B. Handley, *If Truth Were a Child: Essays*

Melissa Wei-Tsing Inouye, *Crossings: A Bald Asian American Latter-day Saint Woman Scholar's Ventures through Life, Death, Cancer & Motherhood (Not Necessarily in That Order)*

George B. Handley, *The Hope of Nature: Our Care for God's Creations*

James E. Faulconer, *Thinking Otherwise: Theological Explorations of Joseph Smith's Revelations*

Samuel M. Brown, *Where the Soul Hungers: One Doctor's Journey from Atheism to Faith*

Charels Shirō Inouye, *Zion Earth Zen Sky*

Patrick Q. Mason and J. David Pulsipher, *Proclaim Peace: The Restoration's Answer to an Age of Conflict*

THE
DOORS
OF
FAITH

TERRYL GIVENS

BYU
Maxwell
Institute

DESERET
BOOK

No portion of this book may be reproduced by any means or process without the formal written consent of the publisher. Direct all permissions requests to: MIpermissions@byu.edu

The paper used in this publication meets the minimum requirements of the American National Standards for Information Sciences—Permanence of Paper for Printed Library Materials. ANSI Z39.48-19

ISBN: 978-0-8425-0055-5

Library of Congress Control Number: 2021943340

(CIP data on file)

Cover design: Heather Ward

Cover image "Arches Corridor" by SVPanteon used under license from Shutterstock.com

Printed in the United States of America

http://maxwellinstitute.byu.edu

To Clay Newberry
Usque ad aras amicus

CONTENTS

The Mortality
of Mortality

by John Rosenberg

Our eternal selves are veterans of transitions. Thresholds.
Awakenings. Of these, mortality is the transition most remembered because it is the one saturated with anxiety of the
unremembered intentionally.

Young adults who go away to college enter a mortality of their mortality: they leave home and their parents'
nurture; they come to an alien place; they are tested and
proved (Abr. 3:25); and they make decisions that, while
not irreversible, are pivotal in shaping a future that exceeds
all imaginings. As Terryl Givens explains in the pages that
follow, proving involves gaining "certain knowledge by
the operation of something on ourselves." The operations
active during the mortality of mortality are common and
nearly universal, yet they are experienced by each as something unique and peculiar and intensely personal. They are
the source of anxiety and the catalyst of questions; they are
planned and purposeful.

Anxiety-bathed questions often involve wonderings

about what was learned before the transition to the university, about the trajectory of the plot of the plan of happiness, and about the role one chooses (or is called) to play. Some seemingly resolve these questions effortlessly. Others wrestle, like Jacob with the angel, and come up lame, still seeking a blessing.

Love for the wrestlers led to an invitation to Givens to offer a series of lectures at Brigham Young University during the fall of 2019. Faculty, staff, and administrators at BYU (as at other schools of faith) keenly feel the privilege and the weight of serving as students' guides as they navigate the mortality of their mortality. Dr. Givens's monthly lectures delivered to a full hall over the course of a semester encouraged students to "choose to believe" and at the same time fortified those students' guides. *The Doors of Faith* is a reworking and compilation of those lectures. Though originally conceived as a balm and guide for university students, this book is for all who recognize the need for refreshing and relearning—whatever their age or circumstance.

Doors are transitional spaces, thresholds to be crossed, pasts to be transcended, undetermined futures to be glimpsed with faith: "it doth not yet appear what we shall be." Other doors mark home, a returning and reaffirming: "but we know that, when he shall appear, we shall be like him" (1 John 3:2). This book is a primer for travelling between those two doors of faith—between the first door of leaving and questing and proving and the second door of arrival in the encircling arms of safety (Alma 34:16).

This book falls in the tradition of gospel manuals like those produced decades ago by B. H. Roberts or Hugh Nibley. Skimming and glancing will not do; one won't find tweeted answers to obvious questions. Hovering makes sense here or savoring—the sitting and pondering common to Nephi and Joseph F. Smith (1 Ne. 11:1; D&C 138:1). Professor Givens invites you on a journey; it is your spiritual and intellectual companionship that interests him, a deep engagement with ideas and covenants—a conversation and a conversion.

This is a book of "perhaps," "what if," and wonderings (in both senses of that word). Watch carefully and you will encounter those words frequently: "perhaps life's task is to discover . . . ," "perhaps we are set adrift . . . ," "what if a second meaning lies concealed?," "you might wonder," and "open to wonderment." Openness to the unfamiliar or the unknown is not a betrayal of what we know or have done. It is *sine qua non* of continuing learning and becoming. Un-openness is the delusion of self-sufficiency and a capitulation to complacency; to be open is to confess our perpetual neediness and to embrace our infinite perfectability. Openness positioned on the threshold of the doors of faith fears not what might be learned because it finds companionship in the fallibility of all and safety in the infallibility of the One. Givens discovers in Joseph Smith a paragon of openness through the Prophet's "insatiable appetite in his attempt to penetrate the veils of heaven and of history, [in] the intellectual and spiritual energies with which he pursued his task, and [in] his indifference to the uneven results of his own ongoing and ever incomplete explorations."

Givens does not claim to offer the final word on any of the boundless subjects he addresses; he doesn't even claim that this book is *his* final word on those matters. A claim to that kind of finality would be arrogant, and it would declare the quest complete. Similarly, Givens claims only the authority derived from his efforts, intellectual discipline, and intimate spiritual inquiries. The right to declare doctrine belongs to others, and Givens is as loyal to (and as grateful for) living prophets as he is for Joseph. Modeling the openness he hopes his readers will pursue, he looks for light wherever he can find it: in the pages of the *Ensign* and from modern and ancient scripture but also from a painting, or the song of an unusual bird, or in the stones of a cathedral, or the writings of the earliest Christians, or in colloquy with his remarkable wife.

Givens reads, and converses, and writes partly because he finds the topics he addresses so interesting but mostly because he knows they are *everything*, or at least a subset of everything, that ultimately matters. "Embracing Jesus Christ and his gospel," Givens reminds us, "provides us with the most *morally* compelling, *intellectually* satisfying, and *aesthetically* appealing account of the universe and our place in it" (my emphases). In so writing, he recognizes an echo of the classical striving for the good, the true, and the beautiful. As it turns out, these interesting things that matter also caught Brigham Young's attention in crafting his definition of the ends of education: "Education is the power to think clearly, the power to act well in the world's work, and the power to appreciate life."[1] Think clearly—our intellectual capacity (the glory of God is intelligence), act well—our moral vocation (the living sacrifice of "reasonable service" [Rom. 12:1]), appreciation—our aesthetic sense (seek anything lovely). These are the coordinates of a liberal education and the curriculum of mortality's mortality.

Givens is a literary critic, a theologian, a philosopher,

a historian, but it is not the abstractions of these fields that motivate him ("Theology, to the ears of many, moves us away from the demands of practical religion"); it is the experience of hearing and responding to the "call of love," and it is love that motivates the pilgrim to quest toward and beyond the doors of faith. It is love (not duty) that motivates service to fellow travelers, especially the kind of service that offers not only a helping hand but a healing heart (Mosiah 2:17); it is healing service that introduces us to and aligns us with the heart of the Master, bringing us to a knowledge of his nature and the nature of his service (Mosiah 5:13); it is that knowledge of the Master and his Father that opens the doors of eternal life (John 17:3); it is the gift of immortality and eternal life that is (not only was) the work and the glory of him who demonstrated "no greater love" (John 15:13). Openness to the unfamiliar, the strange, the alien, the unexpected is prologue and preparation for openness to divine love that transfigures al-one into at-one—loneliness to "oneing" (or perhaps it is the other way around or both at the same time).

• "Life is an upper-division course in gradual sanctification," Givens writes, and "if life is a school, then we must trust the schoolmaster." And so it is with the mortality of mortality: straining, stretching, stumbling, stammering, grasping the rod and recovering the grasp, remembering and taming the anxiety of the unremembered. An Eton schoolmaster in the nineteenth century asked his students not to despair over the unremembered, "for the shadow of lost knowledge . . . protects you from many illusions."[2] Perhaps that lost knowledge—the intimations of immortality (in Wordsworth's phrasing, "The things which I have seen

I now can see no more"[3])—are pre-existent shadows; perhaps it is the counsels and stories of a more recent home; perhaps the shadow of lost knowledge is what is retained after this semester's finals—the dispositions of wonder and teachability; perhaps it is what little you remember a year or two after reading this book. A shadow by day—not a bad thing that.

Terryl and Fiona Givens, friends for forty years (an exodus of time), are fellow wanderers and wonderers—and messengers of healing to my family and me. They have mourned with us, comforted us, born burdens with us. They strive to know and then imitate the source of healing: the God who weeps, the Christ who heals, the Refiner of the crucible of doubt. This most recent offering is an invitation to find reasons to hope (1 Pet. 3:15), to make the "willing and witting" choice to believe, and to contribute to the fellowship of the fragile finding their way home.

Introduction[1]

Why is it so hard to believe? Why, believing, is it so hard to remain constant in that faith? Why a veil, obscuring from us our origins, our true home, the reality of a living God?

THE COMPASS

Anxiety appears to be the default human condition. We are fragile creatures, and at the best of times, we have a tenuous hold on happiness. We are anxious about loved ones, about the state of our world, about our work, our health, and the ineradicable burden of measuring up to our own hopes and expectations. Even those secure in their discipleship find all too few moments of respite from a world strewn with reminders of our vulnerability, the brittleness of life. Anxiety is more than a drain on our body and soul; it short-circuits the flourishing that we are here to cultivate in ourselves and engender in others. The great Reinhold Niebuhr wrote that "without freedom from anxiety man is so enmeshed in the vicious circle of egocentricity, so concerned about himself that he cannot release himself for the adventure of love."[2] A single mother in her distress came to

1

me as her bishop. Fatigued, falling short of her own expectations as a mother, and angry at the lack of mentoring and ministering the ward provided for her son, she half railed and half pled: "Where is the support I desperately need? Why is no one helping me?" I mentally reviewed again the list of members of a weak and struggling ward. There were simply more souls in crisis than there were hands to succor. It struck me forcefully—from that pained perspective—that rare is the individual who awakes in the morning, finds his or her reservoirs of emotional, physical, and spiritual waters brimming, and says, "To whom shall I bestow the superabundance of my energies and resources today?" Would that that were the case; alas, the truth is otherwise.

Niebuhr's "adventure of love" may be the grandest consequence of a life of faith, though little noted. Faith liberates us from the angst of our own preoccupations and frees us to listen, to fully attend, to clearly see the other. And so it may even be the case that as our aptitude for and exercise of faith increases, so does our capacity for what Clement of Rome called "the practice of love."[3] Most of us do not fall neatly into categories of belief and nonbelief, perfect faith and debilitating anxiety. Faith occupies a spectrum, as does the degree of our other-directedness. None of us has yet reached that perfect day when we see as we are seen. That is why the nurturing of faith is an incremental task that beckons to us all.

Then why so many impediments to a life of confident belief? As Saints, we are often directed to the explanation that we must be tested, that if we could remember our heavenly home and see those divine beings who preside there, finding certitude in our purpose and destiny, life would constitute no test. A moment's reflection will suffice to show the inadequacy of such an explanation; common though it may be in our Church culture, it doesn't really hold up. We all know persons who harbor no doubts at all, some whose faith is so absolute, so natural and inevitable, that they confidently and truly say on any given fast Sunday, "I *know* the Church is true. I *know* God lives." And listening, we know that for some of them at least, they speak truly. And yet, the lives of such persons are no easier, their challenges no fewer, their trials no less meaningful or fruitful. No, knowledge of the truth does not in and of itself short-circuit the process of moral formation and spiritual growth. So we start again:

> *Why is it so hard to believe? And why, believing,*
> *is it so hard to remain constant in that faith?*

When I was a scout, I had an old-school compass. Not the one on the smartphone—the kind with a real needle. It wasn't always easy to get a reading. You had to hold it perfectly level or the needle would hang up on the glass casing. You had to hold it steady or the needle kept jiggling around. Perfectly still, perfectly level, perfectly unimpeded by wind or drafts within its glass enclosure, the needle could at last swing free and find its true north. That was always a satisfying moment: The needle's atoms are in perfect alignment in their domains, the domains lined up in the same direction, producing a magnetic field. And in properly sheltered calm and equipoise, that nature is revealed, and the needle moves assuredly, confidently, toward the greater invisible force without.

The analogy is not exact. We are not born into a condition of sheltered stillness. Quite the contrary. We come with massive inherited baggage, multiple influences on our bodies and psyches, inherited predispositions, innate biological needs, inflicted emotional wounds, and fleshly appetites and weaknesses. We are in the maelstrom, not safe under hermetically sealed glass.

And yet, something in us is "whole from the foundation of the world."[4] And perhaps life's task is to discover, and to express, an authentic self that emerges out of all those forces and distractions. To find, if not utter stillness, at least a kind of self-knowledge, a stable fixed point from which we at last act rather than merely live to be acted upon. Our foundational story tells us that the world was created so that God could "prove [us] herewith."[5] However, my mind recoils at the specter of a God hiding himself from us to see if we will obey in the absence of fear, like a child left with a cupcake and a hidden camera to test her mettle. The 1828 Webster's dictionary suggests a magnificent alternative to our reading of Abraham 3:25. "Prove," the term's very first entry explains, means "to ascertain some unknown quality . . . by an experiment." Webster elaborates: "To experience . . . to gain certain knowledge by the operation of something on ourselves."[6] Now that is an undertaking to embrace rather than resent.

Perhaps we are set adrift in this world of obscurity and turmoil and trial so that we can fight our way through to genuine self-knowledge, finding a way to let our compass needle swing free amidst the din. And in that discovery, we may find a way forward, to cultivate and nourish and expand that "unknown quality" that hides within. Why the difficulty? Why so much pain and injury along the route?

4

FRAGILITY

The writer Nassim Taleb coined a new word to fill a void in our thinking about the concept of fragility. He notes that we usually think of its opposite as "sturdy" or "unbreakable." But as he points out, the opposite of breakable is not unbreakable, just as the opposite of diseased is not healthy, nor is the opposite of broken, repaired. In all such cases, one is countering a negative with a neutral. The word we lack is *antifragile*. As he explains, "Antifragility is beyond resilience or robustness. The resilient resists shock and stays the same; the antifragile gets better." Many things in the world—the inanimate particularly—are merely robust. Living, vital things are more likely to be antifragile. "The antifragile loves randomness and uncertainty, which also means—crucially—a love of errors. . . . Antifragility has a singular property of allowing us to deal with the unknown, to do things without understanding them—and do them well."[7] Taleb's background is in finance and risk analysis, but his insight seems particularly relevant to matters of ultimate concern:

> Consider that Mother Nature is not just "safe." It is aggressive in destroying and replacing, in selecting and reshuffling. When it comes to random events, "robust" is certainly not good enough. In the long run everything with the most minute vulnerability breaks, given the ruthlessness of time—yet our planet has been around for perhaps four billion years and, convincingly, robustness can't just be it: you need perfect robustness for a crack not to end up crashing the system. Given the unattainability of

perfect robustness, we need a mechanism by which the system regenerates itself continuously by using, rather than suffering from, random events, unpredictable shocks, stressors, and volatility.[8]

Neuroscience provides confirmation that as human beings, we are specifically designed, our brains are actually constructed, in such a way that they maximize unexpected input for our ultimate growth and advantage. David Eagleman writes that "our machinery isn't fully preprogrammed, but instead shapes itself by interacting with the world. As we grow, we constantly rewrite our brain's circuitry to tackle challenges, leverage opportunities, and understand the social structures around us."[9] One can sense the deep eternal principle underlying these scientific discoveries about our incompleteness, our seeming fragility and ill-suitedness to the stresses and randomness of life. It turns out that something beyond mere Darwinian survival is unfolding:

We represent the highest expression of a trick that Mother Nature discovered: don't entirely pre-script the brain; instead, just set it up with the basic building blocks and get it into the world. The bawling baby eventually stops crying, looks around, and absorbs the world around it. . . . It soaks up everything from local language to broader culture to global politics. . . . Every fond memory it possesses, every lesson it learns, every drop of information it drinks— all these fashion its circuits to develop something that was never pre-planned.[10]

These two principles, the compass and fragility, frame—or found, really—the four chapters that follow, establishing what I believe are two nonnegotiable dimensions of faith. The compass needle illustrates our predicament. It does not always align simply, automatically, in a useful direction. Our inner world is as chaotic as the outer. Are we hearing the call of conscience or the phantoms of wishful thinking? Is my anxiety the pangs of guilt or the leftovers of repressive upbringing? Is the Church making me into a little Christ or a little robot?[11] Am I being gullible or faithful? We are utterly, indissolubly products of our culture, our history, our upbringing. We cannot extricate ourselves from our situatedness in time and place and relationship, so how can we ever hope to see the compass needle swing free? It is my impression that we seldom achieve such moments of sublime, perfect transcendence; though, poets and mystics alike have written about such escape from the dross of a material world. Wordsworth, for example, thought he had glimpsed

> that blessed mood,
> In which the burthen of the mystery,
> In which the heavy and the weary weight
> Of all this unintelligible world,
> Is lightened:—that serene and blessed mood,
> In which the affections gently lead us on.[12]

But my assumption behind these reflections is that most of us never—or seldom—find that place outside any place, the moment outside of all time when we know, as C. S. Lewis hoped to know, with serene certainty that it is "the real I" communicating with "the real Thou."[13] Our predicament requires that we reinscribe faith into our religious vocabulary. We must confront the unavoidable necessity for faith, and make sure we understand what the term means and does not mean. Faith is not a conjecture about the possible. It is not a wishful, desperate hope about what may exist. It is our response to that reality in which we are always already immersed. It is a risk-laden gesture of trust. This is why arguments about religious beliefs are never effective. I cannot persuade you to have an experience of truth. I can offer you a hypothesis against which you measure your own experience. That is all.

But the fragility of our predicament is necessary to foster flourishing. Only when incomplete souls encounter a world of unpredictable novelty are we forced to engage that world with creativity and risk. As Eagleman summarizes, "Build [or start] incompletely and let world experience refine." An environment in perpetual "flux" is the requirement for an organism to "actively improve, self-adjust," and "optimize its efficacy."[14]

With those principles in mind, a word about what follows. I intend simply to play some of the music that has been background to whatever equipoise I have found as an aspiring disciple. From the most rigorous calculations, we know that there is overwhelming evidence that we cannot detect 95% of the physical universe. Dark matter and dark energy are neither perceptible nor observable by any scientific instrument or human faculty. Yet unless we posit their existence, the equations we use to make sense of what we can observe don't work. Similarly, although we can't detect spiritual realities directly, the life I experience doesn't make sense without acknowledging that another plane of existence is there, like dark matter and dark energy, threaded through the fibers of space and time.

We cannot live without these frameworks, these narratives we construct. Consider your own life and the sense you make of it. It is not just a future biographer who would have to select from the infinite details of your life, from the countless thoughts and actions, experiences and witnessings, inclinations and triumphs to tell your life story. You, too, at every waking moment, are living the story you choose to tell yourself that gives coherence, purpose, meaning to your existence. You are not just an object among objects in an endless stream of cause and effect. You choose and navigate, or you meander and drift—but in every case, witting or not, you consolidate a limited set of data points to constitute a story with you as the protagonist. We could not rise from one day to the next and engage the tempests of life without this most fundamental place of beginning: I have a life, and this is my story.

The account the Restoration gives, the stories it tells, the world before and after this one that it describes, and the agencies it reveals all pertain to a larger, more complete plane of existence. Most significant of all, the God and Christ it describes cause the world of my own experience to fall into focus and make rational, aesthetic, and moral sense.

CHAPTER 1

A WILLING
AND WITTING
DISCIPLESHIP

We are all at various stages in our faith journey, and our places on the path span a wide range. Faith commitments, or what we generally call testimonies in our culture, come in many flavors. Some disciples are attracted by the data. After all, Saints have longer lives, better health, fewer divorces, and more reported happiness.[1] Some stay for the community. Descended from pioneer stock or enmeshed in the all-pervading bonds of ward life, one's identity as part of this people becomes an almost irresistible bond. Perhaps you find yourself a disciple by inheritance or by inertia. Or maybe spiritual promptings have brought you to this place. Some of you find yourselves in the valley of decision, weighing evidence, pros and cons. As in a marriage, one's motivation behind a whole-souled commitment will shape the quality—and the durability—of that commitment.

In the Christian world and among our fellow Latter-day

Saints, many are choosing, in John's words, to "[walk] no more with [us]."[2] The numbers are heartbreaking. Many and varied are the causes, and all are to be lamented. I am going to propose, as one explanation for what is happening among our own community, the words of the poet Thomas Traherne: "No man . . . that clearly seeth the beauty of God's face . . . can when he sees it clearly, willingly, and wittingly forsake it."[3] These words have become scripture to me: "No man . . . that clearly seeth the beauty of God's face . . . can when he sees it clearly, willingly, and wittingly forsake it."

There is a love of Christ known to medieval Saints and mystics; there is a devotion to the Savior that has carried many to their martyrdom. There is a love of Christ that has led one of the God-touched to comfort a solitary woman in her grief and another disciple to reshape the history of civilization. Such a love is transformative. Some of you, through grief and heartache, have felt the Savior's embrace, the stirrings of a personal gratitude, and a transforming love. Gregory of Nazianzus, a fourth-century voice of light, did. He portrayed in his most beautiful sermon a visual account of the Savior's ministry. His reason for following the Christ comes through clearly and poignantly: In his imagined retelling, "[Jesus] teacheth, now on a mountain; now He discourseth on a plain; now He passeth over into a ship; now He rebuketh the surges. And perhaps He goes to sleep, in order that He may bless sleep also; . . . perhaps He weeps that He may make tears blessed." Continuing on, Gregory sees in his mind's eye the Savior as he approaches his earthly suffering: "He endureth all things. . . . He put up with blows, He bore spittings, He tasted gall. . . ." Abruptly,

Gregory breaks off because he is overcome with the feeling that he is not worthy to put into human language this incomprehensible being and his incomprehensible sacrifice: "And pardon me meanwhile that I again suffer a human affection. I am filled with indignation and grief for my Christ (and I would that you might sympathize with me) when I see my Christ dishonored on this account on which He most merited honor."[4]

I believe Traherne is correct, that no one who sees the beauty of God's face can willingly and wittingly forsake him. If that is true—yet everywhere we turn, men and women *are* "willingly forsaking the beauty of God's face"—then perhaps the choices are not being made "wittingly." Perhaps too many of us never came to fully know and see what Traherne—and Gregory—knew and saw and therefore loved. The poet John Milton wrote that if one believes because "his pastor says so . . . without knowing other reason, *though his belief be true, yet the very truth he holds becomes his heresy*";[5] John Stuart Mill issued a parallel warning: "There is a class of persons . . . who think it enough if a person assents undoubtingly to what they think true, though he has no knowledge whatever of the grounds of the opinion. . . . This is not knowing the truth. Truth, thus held, is but *one superstition the more, accidentally clinging to the words which enunciate a truth*" (my emphases).[6] Milton and Mill, like Traherne, are making the same point: we may hold the truth but hold it with insufficient understanding, appreciation, or intimacy; we may give it our assent without giving it our hearts; or we may know the correct facts about Christ and his Restoration without having experienced the Christ and his gospel. When Adam and Eve "knew" each other, they experienced each other in the most complete, total, immersive intimacy of which humans are capable.[7] When the angel asked Nephi if he "knew" the condescension of God, he was clearly referring to more than an intellectual apprehension.[8] He wanted to know if Nephi had been remade by the experience of Christ's absolute compassion, the stunning realization of Christ's shared suffering in our pain. Had he lived through what Alma referred to as a "mighty change" that impels one to "sing the song of redeeming love"?[9]

Declarations at the pulpit, expressing the familiar pattern of "I know," are but shallow imitations of such intimate encounters that remake us and bring us face to face with a world, a life, and a God endowed with their true identity. One of Christianity's first great apologists, Irenaeus, recognized the importance of reasoned argument in sustaining faith. Ultimately, however, he said Christ's purpose was to effect an atonement—that is, a reconciliation, a union— of humans and God. And that union, that at-one-ing, is already unfolding under the transformative reality of the Spirit that brings us into communion with God. It is in the face of this reality—a lived transformation one can see at work in the life of his disciples—that the gospel of Jesus Christ finds its irrefutable witness. In the face of these lived, experienced, discernible truths, "all the doctrines" of the doubters "fall to ruin."[10] The rationality of faith is nowhere more evident than its lived efficacy.

Traherne is suggesting that our devotion to the Savior and Healer of the world may be thought of as having two components: a willing heart and a witting mind. Since that latter expression is crucial but perhaps unfamiliar, a definition is called for. A witting mind is one that is conscious, fully aware, rooted in the requisite knowledge. I want to link the two concepts of wit and will together in this way: Anything short of a fervent love for Jesus Christ, any belief structure that is not predicated on a profound and personal response to him—a living, trusting response—is sure to fail us in the end. The seeds of that response must be sown in the soil of correct understanding. The deepest levels of devotion can only be stirred by our full understanding of the Other. However, it is not knowledge alone, taught the mystic Emanuel Swedenborg, but love that kindles the will.[11]

We may begin with habit, duty, fear of hell or hope of heaven. But the only durable discipleship is rooted in the capacity to feel and reciprocate the love of Christ. Such love is the final stage of the disciple's journey. The problem with institutional religion—even one divinely restored—is the temptation it affords us to make our own spirituality the goal. Rules, standards, and commandments all provide us with the means of measuring our own progress, our own prospects for happiness. That is not discipleship—it is pious self-interest, little different in motivation than Pascal's infamous wager,[12] and it is a plant that will not bloom.

> DURABLE DISCIPLESHIP IS ROOTED IN THE CAPACITY TO FEEL AND RECIPROCATE THE LOVE OF CHRIST.

But how to develop the kind of love that we seek? The love that has fired the hearts of Christ's most fervent and steadfast disciples is not easily acquired. One of the wisest of Proverbs counsels us that if we "commit [our] works unto the Lord, [our] thoughts shall be established."[13] Great hope can emerge from those words because they assure us that the purest love and transcendent motives to which we aspire may come after a life of disciplined, effortful striving. That is why Moroni urges us that we must pray "with all the energy of heart" to obtain it;[14] why, as President Benson urged, we must make faithfulness to his counsel a quest;[15] why, as King Benjamin observed, we cannot know the master we have not served;[16] why, as Alma counseled his son, we must learn to place all "the affections of [our] heart" upon him.[17] Finally, it is why, as the Cambridge Platonist John Smith recognized, "that which enables us to know and understand aright the things of God, must be a living principle of holiness within us."[18] Prayerful seeking, a questing faithfulness, consistent service, disciplined desire, holiness—all these are indispensable elements of a love of Christ, which love is the only sure foundation. They are not my focus at present, though each one deserves a sermon of its own. I want to develop another foundation for a love-based discipleship, implied by Traherne's reference to a "witting" devotion—that is, a devotion steeped in a thoughtful, reflective, and perceptive awareness. A knowing love. Perhaps this fulsome knowledge is what is entailed in the scriptural key that knowing God is life eternal.[19]

Think of the times in your life that you learned a deeper truth about a person you knew—maybe it was a person you loved. But as further aspects of that person's life, or goodness, or suffering were revealed to you, your love deepened. I served a mission many years ago, using money I had conscientiously saved from a young age. But it ran out before my term of service did. Still, the money kept coming in.

Only later did I learn that my mother had taken a job as a custodian, cleaning the local chapel every week, to secure the funds that saw me through my mission. Can you imagine the deepening of my love for a mother willing to quietly render such anonymous kindness to her son? My love was enlarged by a deeper understanding of her love.

I am not a saint, and I am not a mystic. But I have devoted many years to the study of Joseph Smith's teachings and revelations. And as my comprehension of God's nature, his attributes, and his designs for the human family have grown, so has my love for him and for his Son. So I will be sharing a testimony of what I hope is my witting love for the Savior. By that, I mean to suggest that we can come to a greater love of the Lord as we become more aware, more understanding, more reflective, and more informed about just what the Restoration of his gospel entails. It is more remarkable and more revolutionary than we may have perceived.

In the pages that follow, I will share my conviction that embracing Jesus Christ and his gospel provides us with the most morally compelling, intellectually satisfying, and aesthetically appealing account of the universe and our place in it and that such a knowledge is a powerful catalyst to a love—a witting love—of Christ that will endure.

Restoration teachings usher us into a world in which all things are new.[20] What happens when we pass through these doors of faith? According to Luke, the Lord, through the apostle Paul, had "opened the door of faith unto the Gentiles."[21] Paul's role in Christian history was to restore covenantal understanding to its primeval intent: an invitation that extended its purview to encompass the entirety of the human family—Jew and Gentile, all are alike unto God.[22]

All may come and freely partake. That was the revolution ushered in by Paul. The doors of faith were now open to all.

But what if a second meaning lies concealed in Paul's words—a meaning that heralds a revolution equally profound but more intimate, more personal. The words *door of faith*, in Luke's sense, may well signify a moment when all are now free to pass through a gate into a new arena. After all, doors normally open to let us in. I want to argue for an equally potent but opposite meaning of these words. Only when something has been disturbed in our own minds are we open to new possibilities coming toward us. Perhaps the most important doors that had to be opened were not the gates of Church membership; perhaps they were the closed doors shaped by our own preconceptions. The power and potency of our faith is that it collapses sacred distances, fills the empty tomb with concrete artifacts, materializes angels, and furnishes heaven with familiar furniture. It is other worldly and this worldly because it draws all things together. By so doing, it shows the efficacy of faith in remaking the here and now.

I take the doors of faith to refer to the world to which we are now fully open. Immersion in the lived reality of Latter-day Saint teachings remaps our universe, and by so doing, it turns us from wandering trekkers into purposeful pilgrims. It rescripts the narrative and transforms us from characters in someone else's play (Freud's? Darwin's? Nietzsche's?) into living, breathing selves with a deep history and a real family. Entering through the doors of faith, we conceive an origin in heaven raised by Heavenly Parents. We interpret our travails here as an intended immersion in an earthly school of love with Christ as our ever-present Healer and Comforter. And we live with hope and confidence in our Heavenly Parents' desire and capacity to guide us into full heirship with them and lasting communion with all those we hold dear.

This willful, deliberate act of faith becomes the portal into an ampler reality, not a profession of tenuous conjectures. The test of any religious claim has to be measured in the real world, more particularly, in how it enriches—gives real heft to—our life in that world. Not in some self-satisfied, subjective way. I am not saying that if it makes us feel good, let's buy into it. I am saying that religion must be enacted and not merely thought or believed. And in the lived experience of this new truth, oneself is realigned. One passes from a world of surfaces and appearances into a reality of hard, sharp contours.

In C. S. Lewis's *Perelandra*, the character Ransom is confronted by an angel, and to his utter confusion, his reality is not simply invaded by an alien presence; on the contrary, the most unexpected consequence is that his whole frame of reference shifts, and for a moment, he grasps that his entire orientation had always been out of alignment. In a moment, this old, trusted frame of reference utterly dissolves:

> What one actually felt at the moment was that the column of light was vertical but the floor was not horizontal—the whole room seemed to have heeled over as if it were on board ship. The impression, however produced, was that this creature had reference to some horizontal, to some whole system of directions, based outside the Earth, and that its mere presence imposed that alien system on me and abolished the terrestrial horizontal.[23]

The scriptural record is replete with allusions to these moments of splendid irony when one awakens into, rather than from, the world's deep reality. For instance, it was *after* his vision that Joseph "came to [him]self," *after* Saul's vision that "there fell from his eyes as it had been scales," *after* their conversion that Alma's converts "awoke unto God," and so forth[24]—"a shock of awful consciousness," in the poet Wordsworth's language.[25] There is enormous distance between assent to propositional claims and a truth fully lived when we open the doors of faith.

To open the doors of faith is to multiply possibilities, to give all options their due, to reclaim a child's open-eyed delight in a world ever full of surprises we could not possibly anticipate. It is to find your soul capacious enough, like Enoch's, to swell wide as eternity.[26] That is what is at stake in embracing Restoration Christianity. Our spiritual eyes awaken, our moral faculties expand, our intellect is unfettered, the veil dissipates, and our capacity to live—here and now, a more abundant life—opens before us. I will try to make explicit and substantive these several claims.

The absolute worst thing we could do, in the aftermath of discoveries that challenge our faith or shatter our comfortable world, is to retreat into an even more protected shelter. It would be as if, seeing our outer walls cast down and stormed, we flee to the innermost, impregnable tower—what Eugene England so memorably called "the appalling luxury of . . . skepticism."[27] Safe we may be, but the tower that has no windows to let in the arrows cannot let in the light either. Mere skepticism in the face of those claims that give definition and meaning to our existence is not a decision—it is a flight from the most urgent questions we can face.

It is helpful in the life of discipleship to begin with a healthy dose of epistemological humility. Physics and cosmology alike can be particularly useful in this regard. The scientist R. Buckminster Fuller wrote that "since the initial publication of the electromagnetic spectrum, humans have learned that what they can touch, smell, see, and hear is less than one-millionth of reality."[28] Another writer points out that the rainbow we perceive on a sunny, rainy day is only ".0035 percent of the electromagnetic spectrum. . . . On either side of it are the invisible wavelengths that we are not biologically equipped to see."[29] There are, however, exceptions to this fact. A condition called tetrachromacy afflicts—or we might say, blesses—a small number of humans. People with this genetic condition "are born with four different cone cells for color vision whereas most of us have three. This fourth receptor allows them to perceive ninety-nine million more shades and hues than the average eye perceives." Yet another condition is called aphakia, Latin for "no lenses." As a consequence of surgery or a birth defect, one or both lenses is absent. One of the functions of the lens of the human eye is to filter out UV light. Without that lens, the person so affected can see UV light, invisible to the rest of us.[30]

What do such conditions teach us? They remind us, as Maria Popova has written, that

> we navigate the world by our common-sense perception, but that perception has blinded us to reality again and again. We have mistaken our sensorial intuitions for facts about the universe—for millennia, we held wrong beliefs about Earth's shape,

motion, and position, because it feels flat and static beneath our feet, and central to the order of the cosmos. We have mistrusted processes and phenomena beyond the boundaries of what we can touch and feel with our limited senses—from evolution, which unfolds on scales too vast to be visible within a human lifetime, to quantum mechanics, which operates on subatomic scales imperceptible and almost inconceivable to the human observer.[31]

The conclusion that science writer Ziya Tong draws from these examples is one with profound import for all of us who engage the challenge of faith in a secular world: "To see the world clearly," she writes, "we must first become aware of the veil; we must recognize our blind spots."[32]

I would like to translate that insight into two propositions regarding what I have called the doors of faith. The first is an epistemological claim, a claim about how we come to know anything. And the second is a philosophical claim about the nature of belief and choice.

First proposition: The gospel opens our faculties— intellectual, moral, and sensory—to the richness of a boundless universe. There are multiple ways of knowing, and we need to honor them all.

The scientist Werner Heisenberg once stated that what we observe in the universe is "not Nature itself but Nature exposed to our method of questioning."[33] Why is that important? Because it tells us how important our questions are. Some questions constrain and limit understanding by their implicit assumptions. And some are generative of insight, empathy, and expansive possibilities. For example, as astrophysicist Marcelo Gleiser elaborates, "Our view of the world is based only on the fraction of reality that we can measure and analyze. Science, as our narrative describing what we see and what we conjecture exists in the natural world, is thus necessarily limited, telling only part of the story."[34]

Faith in something beyond these material realities is so interwoven into our lived experience of the world that we often miss it. In most of life's greatest transactions, where the stakes are the highest, it is to the heart that we rightly turn although not in utter isolation from the rational and reasonable. But whom to marry, what vocation to pursue, when to let go of a dream, what sacrifices to make and promises to keep—these are decisions best made when emotion is moderated but not displaced entirely by logic or rationality alone. And these decisions are certainly made not in the absence of truth but in recognizing those very truths that logic and science may be powerless to detect. To take one of the most important instances of this fact, we may look to the insight of the philosopher William Luijpen. He points out that "we must consider love as an attitude by means of which certain aspects of reality become visible. The true meaning of the

> IN MOST OF LIFE'S GREATEST TRANSACTIONS, WHERE THE STAKES ARE THE HIGHEST, IT IS TO THE HEART THAT WE RIGHTLY TURN ALTHOUGH NOT IN UTTER ISOLATION FROM THE RATIONAL AND REASONABLE.

other as other, i.e., the meaning of the other as subject, becomes visible only through love. An attitude of preoccupation with ourselves, with our own desires and interests, precludes our access to the true meaning of the other."[35] This is not just metaphoric language. In the most emphatic and urgent meaning of the word, love reveals truth. It does not create the impression of truth; love does not merely endow something with a subjective truth. Love is the only position or emotional disposition from which we become fully aware of the already present reality of the other person as more than a mere object among other objects in a crowded universe.

The philosopher David Hume made his recognition of the limits of rationality one of his most controversial—and inspired—principles: "Reason is, and ought only to be the slave of the passions, and can never pretend to any other office than to serve and obey them."[36] Such a statement is easily taken out of context and ridiculed. But Hume's point was simply this: As moral agents immersed in a world of human relationships and human values, we most appropriately choose and judge and act as human beings whose desires and motivations and bases for action are deeper than and prior to logic. For example, we read of an instance of child abuse, and if we are revolted by such an act of cruelty, it is because it elicits our sense of injustice, our sympathy with the victim, our feeling that something wrong has transpired. If we apply our reason to make sense of the event, it is to forge an argument for what we already know to be true. Our intuition of eternal realities precedes its rational articulation. If we find we are unable to express that truth in the language of science or to find logical support for our moral

24

position, that should not blind us to the reality, the truth, that child abuse is wrong. In such a case as this, our failure to find support in science, logic, rationality, or whatever name we want to give it should not cause us to doubt our intuitive moral faculty. On the contrary, it should cause us to place greater trust in and value upon it. Some values—and their wanton destruction—have, and are universally felt to have, an unqualified claim upon our hearts and minds alike. Conscience has preserved us in our humanity even if other ways of knowing have not. As Frances Young notes, "It is rational to accept the limits of human rationality."[37]

Other truths are experienced and known to us through the instrumentality of art, great music, and great literature. Aesthetic perception is one of the most sublime ways of knowing—of "vital importance," notes one prominent psychologist, "as a guide to what is true, good, and sustaining in the human world of experience."[38] That secular prophet Ralph Waldo Emerson said that "our music, our poetry, our language itself are not satisfactions, but suggestions."[39] Ponder the times in your own life that at a moment in Handel's *Messiah*, looking at Michelangelo's *Pietà*, or reading Victor Hugo's story of the bishop's candlesticks, you sensed a living reality behind the art, greater than the power of speech to express. Physicist David Deutsch has recently criticized the fallacy of thinking that a failure to explain or articulate a principle disproves or impugns the objective reality of that fact. For example, he writes, "It is especially hard to express in words the explanation [for] the beauty of a particular work of art, even if one knows it, because the relevant knowledge is itself not expressed in words." And yet, as he notes, if you were to erase one note from one of Mozart's sublime compositions, say his *Requiem*, and replace it with another random note, the work would be diminished, the beauty scarred, its perfection impaired. You as listener, and Mozart as composer, would know a musical truth has been violated. Though what the principle behind that truth is, neither could say. This principle, Deutsch writes, may "one day be expressible in words."[40] At present, it is only experienced—and loved.

The point in these examples is this: the human impulse toward the sublime and the artist's revelation of the beautiful; love's power to unlock the full splendor of the other, its blinding revelation of the infinite worth of the individual; and conscience with its unwavering response to moral imperatives, its piercing protest against evil and gentle enticement to recognize the good—all these are living proofs that different ways of knowing exist and are necessary to escape the blinding confines of any epistemology that is limited to the strictly material. We employ them, we rely upon them, and we trust in them. As well we should.

A growing chorus of philosophers and cosmologists—including a substantial number of atheists—are finding the universe at both the macro and micro scale too transcendently magnificent and mysterious for reductive and materialistic approaches. To take one example of the latter, Thomas Nagel comments that

> the existence of consciousness is both one of the most familiar and one of the most astounding things about the world. No conception of the natural order that does not reveal it as something to be expected can aspire even to the outline of completeness. And

if physical science, whatever it may have to say about the origin of life, leaves us necessarily in the dark about consciousness, that shows that it cannot provide the basic form of intelligibility for this world.[41]

Carl Jung imagined a primeval time when feeling, sensation, intuition, and thought all dwelt in a harmonious synthesis in the human soul. The certainty of love's transformative power, the stunned apprehension of the beautiful, the indelible reality of moral truths that pierce our soul—are these feelings, sensations, and intuitions not avenues to Truth as invaluable and as irreplaceable as the rationality which we have come to value above all other faculties?

No foundation, however logically or rationally appealing, is self-authenticating. And if only evolutionarily derived, then reason itself offers no promise of truth beyond its own immediate functionality. In simpler terms, if reason only evolved for its survival value, why do we trust it for matters far removed from those needs? The biophysicist Max Delbrück was one of the first to recognize this problem. As he wrote,

Our concrete mental operations are indeed adaptations to the mode of life in which we had to compete for survival a long, long time before science. As such we are saddled with them, just as we are with our organs of locomotion and our eyes and ears. But in science we can transcend them, as electronics transcends our sense organs. Why, then, do the formal operations of the mind carry us so much further? Were those abilities not also matters of biological evolution? If they, too, evolved to let us get along in the cave, how can it be that they permit us to obtain deep insights into cosmology, elementary particles, molecular genetics, number theory? To this question I have no answer.[42]

Philosopher Richard Feldman agrees: the principle of "natural selection" gives us no basis for the emergence of "reliable belief-forming strategies."[43] So either we have no basis for confidence in our ability to ascertain trustworthy facts about reality, or we must root our confidence in something other than logic or rationality alone.

One promising source is suggested by the theologian Dietrich von Hildebrand: "The heart," he writes, "has not been given a real place in philosophy." (By the heart, he means the seat of intuition as distinct from rational knowledge.) It "has never been given a standing comparable to that of the intellect and the will."[44] This is both ironic and illogical, he points out, for the following reason. The very roots of the Western philosophical tradition esteem human happiness as the highest good. But human happiness is experienced in the domain of the heart. We explicitly place the highest valuation upon a desired outcome—an affect-laden condition—that is beyond the grasp or the achievement of logic or intellect alone. And yet along the path that leads there, we place far more confidence in cool rationality than in that same human heart with its moral intuitions, its world-transforming compassion and kindness, its intimations of the sacred. This absurd dichotomy may be culturally rooted, but it is no longer even scientifically defensible. As the eminent biologist Frans de Waal writes, "Emotions are an essential part of our intellect. The idea that they are separate remains so ingrained in full force in many circles."[45]

In sum, as the Book of Mormon states with irrefutable wisdom, "whatsoever is light, is good, because it is discernible, therefore ye must know that it is good." That is the most brilliant course in epistemology ever reduced to one scriptural verse. The real is gauged by an experienced impact and registers in our hearts and minds. The good that is "discernible" is therefore "real" and moves us in the direction of a "knowledge [that is] perfect."[46]

> *Second proposition: We are moral agents,*
> *and hence, belief is a choice. But belief, like life,*
> *is difficult by design.*

There has been no more valuable aid to a diagnosis of the human condition than the story of Eden as clarified in Restoration scripture. In this, the most momentous narrative reconstruction in Christian thought, we encounter two remarkable texts that reveal the poignant truth about our predicament, the most valuable of insights into the pained and wounded nature of our lives here. Eve and Adam discover that the primeval conflict at the heart of our existence as moral agents is that we find ourselves in a universe where we are not primarily embroiled in a titanic struggle between good and evil—we find ourselves in a perpetual, more immersive, more quotidian confrontation with competing, often irreconcilable goods.

Centuries of preachers and theologians trace the story of our race to a simplistic dichotomy: obey or disobey. God or the devil. Submission or rebellion. Eve and Adam having chosen wrongly, we are all now vessels of sin looking for redemption. Only in recent generations has the doctrine of original sin lost its primacy as the cornerstone of Christian self-understanding. Joseph revealed an alternative paradigm in 2 Nephi and the Book of Moses alike—an utterly new version of the story in which Eve's choice launches this educative ascent toward godliness that we call mortality. Here in the narrative of Eden we find two terribly compelling options. Yes, obedience and safety and security in God's presence are presented as one of the choices. But the Restoration narratives are more sympathetic to Eve's perception of the alternative: the beauty of the fruit, its goodness as food, its desirability "to make one wise."[47] Have we perhaps missed this convergence in her mind of the sacred triad of the Good, the Beautiful, and the True as acting upon her with a legitimate appeal fully equal to the alternative?

In this—the foundational story of human life in a new plane of existence—the fundamental position in which we find ourselves is that of facing, front and center, not a blatant choice between good and evil but a wrenching decision to be made between competing sets of the good. The philosopher G. W. F. Hegel believed that this scenario, replicated in myriad artistic narratives, expressed the inescapably tragic nature of the universe. There are very few simple choices. No blueprint gives us easy answers. Life's most wrenching choices are not between right and wrong but between competing demands on our time, our resources, our love, and our loyalty. We inhabit a perpetual ground of tension, and that is central to God's purposes for us. We must absorb the lesson of Eden or our lives will be lived in perpetual dismay.

This reading recalls something that C. S. Lewis wrote in

the midst of World War II, which conflict fell with particular brutality on the people of his homeland. He said, "War creates no absolutely new situation; it simply aggravates the permanent human situation so that we can no longer ignore it. *Human life has always been lived on the edge of a precipice*" (my emphasis).[48]

The permanent human situation has always been life on the edge of a precipice. This is not a cosmic accident or the fruit of primordial misdeeds. Life is difficult by design, as my son likes to say—a crucial precept for engaging in life soberly but also joyfully. This perspective is embedded as a remarkable piece of wisdom in Lehi's blessing to his son Jacob: "And now, behold, if Adam had not transgressed he would not have fallen, but he would have remained in the garden of Eden. And all things which were created must have remained in the same state in which they were after they were created."[49]

How utterly incredible that for Lehi the fate worse than death, the condition that he deplores as an unthinkable option, is perpetual equilibrium, stasis. This revisionist account of Eden celebrates our immersion in pain, difficulty, struggle, and variety of experience. The alternative would be "a compound in one" of "all things," a condition of "no life neither death," meaningless sameness.[50] That is the condition for which opposition is the foil, the rescue. I want to nudge you toward the recognition of one kind of precipice, one state of cognitive dissonance in particular: For the choice in Eden, between two competing alternatives that were equally appealing, is an antitype, a template, for the most momentous choice you will all face—today and recurrently in the future. And that is the choice to believe.

Those of you who have lived among the Saints, at home or in your communities, all know one peculiarity of the Latter-day Saint people: It is the cultural rhetoric of certainty. Every month, we hear speaker after speaker testify of truths that they "know" to be true. Please do not misunderstand what I am about to say. "To some it is [truly] given," as the words of scripture promise, "to know that Jesus Christ is the Son of God,"—and that this is his restored gospel.[51] One of the most glorious promises of the gospel is "that every soul who forsaketh his sins and cometh unto me, and calleth on my name, and obeyeth my voice, and keepeth my commandments, shall see my face and *know* that I am" (my emphasis).[52] Every soul. But certainly, the Spirit blows where it lists—and you may be one to whom that gift has not been bestowed. Or you may be one whose certainties of today become your questions of tomorrow. Please recognize that the Lord refers to the capacity to believe without knowing as a gift as well. In fact, scripture suggests it is the greater gift. To his disciples in both hemispheres, Jesus explicitly stated that they are "more blessed" who believe as an act of faith than those driven to certainty by the evidence.[53] Where is the merit in accepting the inevitable? Whereas choosing to believe is an act of both agency and trust.

The call to faith is a summons to engage the heart, to attune it to resonate in sympathy with principles, values, and ideals that we devoutly hope are true and have reasonable but not certain grounds for believing to be true. I am convinced that there must be grounds for doubt as well as belief in order to render the choice more truly a choice and therefore more deliberate and laden with personal vulnerability and investment. The option to believe must appear on one's personal horizon like the fruit of paradise, perched precariously between sets of demands held in dynamic tension. One is, it would seem, always provided with sufficient materials out of which to fashion a life of credible conviction or dismissive denial. We are acted upon, in other words, by appeals to our personal values, our yearnings, our fears, our appetites, and our egos. What we choose to embrace, to be responsive to, is the purest reflection of who we are and what we love. That is why faith, the choice to believe, is in the final analysis a stance that is positively fraught with moral significance and confronted with what seem equally compelling alternatives; remember that there is something to predispose us to a life of faith or a life of unbelief. There is a heart in these conditions of equilibrium and balance— and only in these conditions of equilibrium and balance, equally "enticed by the one or the other"[54]—that is truly free to choose belief or cynicism, faith or faithlessness.

Why, then, is there more value—given this perfect balance—in believing in the Christ (and his gospel and prophets) than believing in a false deity or in nothing at all? Perhaps because there is nothing in the universe, or in any possible universe, more perfectly good, absolutely beautiful, worthy of adoration, and worthy of emulation than this Christ. And a gesture of belief in that direction, a will manifesting itself as a desire to acknowledge his virtues as the paramount qualities of a divided universe, is a response to the best in us, the best and noblest of which the human soul is capable. A gesture of faith is always freighted with risk and is therefore a witness to the value we place on the object of that faith. Such risk is an act of vulnerability. It is therefore an offering of self that we place on the altar in quest of a possibility that is beautiful enough to deserve the sacrifice.[55]

Trust those subtle intimations you find from whatever waters at which you drink as the language of spirit speaking to spirit. I hope you will have the stubborn feistiness of John Keats. Like so many of his age, Keats was disheartened by institutionalized systems of religion that almost universally emphasized human depravity and inherent guilt while themselves doing more to justify than to alleviate human suffering. But something would not let him give in to despair. As he wrote hopefully to his dying brother, "Yet through all this I see [Christ's] splendour. Even here, though I myself am pursuing the same instinctive course as the veriest human animal you can think of, I am, however young, . . . straining at particles of light in the midst of a great darkness." He continued, that while unsure of his own conclusions, he was confident that a "superior being" could not but be pleased with the struggle put forth to make sense of it all. So at the least, he pled—whether to God or to his brother is unclear—"Give me this credit—Do you not think I strive—to know . . . ? Give me this credit."[56]

And please know this: God has consistently affirmed your agency and created the conditions for its exercise. Cultivate that power. The scholar of early Christianity, Elaine Pagels, writes that this belief was the most fundamental principle to followers of Christ and the most catastrophically lost. "Christian converts of the first three centuries . . . regarded the proclamation of αὐτεξουσία—the moral freedom to rule oneself—as virtually synonymous with 'the gospel.'" Yet in succeeding centuries, sadly, "the message changed."[57]

34

I pray you will awaken to the beauty of a faith freely ventured, freely given. And that with time, you will come to see the beauty of God's face—if you have not already—and never willingly nor wittingly forsake him.

CHAPTER 2

THE NATURE OF GOD AND HUMAN ORIGINS

Beholding a world captivated by the teachings of a damaged scriptural inheritance, Nephi sees the inhabitants as suffering in "a state of awful woundedness."[1] The angel imparting the vision did not draw his attention to human evil or wickedness but to the "state of awful woundedness" in which we dwell, and the angel diagnosed the cause: the loss of the scripture's "plain and precious" truths. It is my contention that the loss of two doctrines in particular and the creedal claims that replaced them explain, at least in part, such pervasive spiritual damage.

More than three decades ago, the Methodist scholar Jan Shipps argued that what she called "Mormonism" constitutes a "new religious tradition."[2] I agree. Not, perhaps, for the reasons she articulated but because of its radical repair of traditional Christian notions of God and of the human. Restoration theology presented the world with something dramatically—but resonantly—different. We have under-appreciated, and therefore insufficiently represented to our people and to the world, just how remarkably Latter-day Saint teachings depart from the views current in 1830. Two teachings in particular establish a distinctively different religious tradition:

1. Heavenly Parents—including a Heavenly Mother—whose vulnerable hearts beat in sympathy with ours, sharing our joys but also our pain.[3]
2. Our soul is eternal, coming from a place of glory.

THE DIVINE NATURE

On that spring day in 1820 when all things were made new, the Lord employed strikingly sharp language to characterize the contemporary religious world to Joseph. "Their creeds were an abomination," he told the young boy.[4] Note, first of all, that this was no condemnation of other Christians; it was an assessment of certain codified statements of belief. Second, note that he did not specify which creeds were the target of his rebuke. However, we can reasonably infer from his subsequent statements which creeds Joseph believed were the target of divine displeasure. Joseph, Warren Cowdery, and Parley Pratt all made reference to the same creedal pronouncements as the source of so many of Christianity's ills.[5] The most influential creed in the Protestant world has been the Westminster Confession of Faith. Approved by the English Parliament in 1648, this creed established the basis of Reformed theology embraced by the Puritans and the Presbyterians. This document served as the basis of Baptist and Congregationalist theology as well, and

Methodists employed the identical language in their Articles of Religion.

The first sentence of the second article states: "There is but one only living and true God, . . . without body, parts, or passions."[6] What does it mean to claim that our God is a Being devoid of passions? The idea that God in some sense is characterized by emotion is clear; to be impassible, however, means that God is not moved, altered, or affected by those emotions. In the words of one authoritative source, "Orthodox theology has traditionally denied God's subjection to . . . feelings of pleasure and pain caused by the action of another being."[7] As Augustine asked almost two millennia ago, "Who can sanely say that God is touched by any misery?"[8] Centuries later, Thomas Aquinas confirmed that "to sorrow . . . over the misery of others belongs not to God."[9]

Some critics insist that impassibility only implies a different kind of feeling in God. To this view, two points are especially germane. First, the consensus of religious scholars is that an enormous shift toward a "suffering God" took place in the late 19th century (see below). Such a shift would have been redundant if a suffering God were already standard orthodoxy in Protestant and Catholic Christianity. Second, what is most relevant is the simple inference that lay Protestants would draw from their creedal language. "Without passions" meant to be without "susceptibility of impressions from external agents," immune to "feeling[s] of the mind, . . . [such] as desire, hope, joy, grief, love" according to an 1828 dictionary.[10] To an audience untutored in the fine distinctions of scholastic theology, the plain meaning of a God devoid of "passions" would undoubtedly have been wounding to millions.

These considerations may help explain why the Lord referred to creedal documents affirming such characterizations of God as "abominations." God—the clear creedal implication is—is moved to no sorrow by your pain. He does not share your sadness, and he is untouched by your loneliness. He persists in perfect equanimity, unfazed by the vicissitudes of your life, as unmoved by your suffering as he is unaffected by your joys. Although medieval writers like the hugely influential theologian Anselm (1033–1109) believed God in his mercy worked to alleviate our suffering, they generally held that he was not himself touched or affected by our pain. In Anselm's words, God "looks upon us in our wretchedness . . . [but] feels not the effect. . . . Saves the wretched, . . . [but] is touched by no fellow-suffering in that wretchedness."[11] Creedal affirmations of this impassible God were made by virtually every Christian denomination on the planet when Joseph entered the Sacred Grove. Doubtless multitudes of Christians, then as now, intuited something closer to the God Joseph would restore.

You might wonder at this point why—in pre-Restoration belief—God would go to the trouble of creating beings whose pain and suffering could not reach his heart. That question has been asked—and answered—numerous times in the history of religious thought. One hundred and fifty years after Christ, Tertullian taught that God "brought forth from nothing this entire mass of our world, with all its array of elements, bodies, spirits, for the glory of His [own] majesty."[12] In the seventeenth century, the English Puritan Thomas Watson asked his congregation, "What is the chief end of man?" and supplied his own answer that "man's chief end is to glorify God."[13] According to the great

American divine Jonathan Edwards, God "always acts for his own glory and honor."[14] The first lesson of the Baltimore Catholic catechism asked, "Why did God make you?" The answer was that "God made me to know him, to love him, and to serve him."[15] This view of God continues into the twenty-first century. One of the most popular preachers of our era writes, "You were made for God's glory."[16] An evangelical author of more than forty books likewise writes that "God loves his own glory above all things."[17]

Most moral philosophers and people of good sense would say that the highest right we have as human beings is to be treated as an "I" and not an "it," a subject and not an object, a person with our own desires, interests, and intentions rather than a means to another person's end. If that is correct, then anything that turns us into an "it," an object, a means or instrument or vehicle of another person's interests or intentions, would be evil. Virtually all human evils can be interpreted in the light of this basic premise. Human trafficking, pornography, theft, fraud, rape—or more subtle evils, such as flattery, high-pressure sales, emotional manipulation—these and a thousand other varieties of wrongdoing objectify and instrumentalize other human beings. What greater perversity could we imagine than to take a human being made in the likeness and image of God and reduce her or him to a mere object among objects, a rung on the ladder of our own self-interest, a stepping-stone on the path to our own self-aggrandizement, or a disposable diversion in our pursuit of a self-serving aim? And yet, suggestions like those above hold that God created the human race as a means to enhancing his own glory. That we should wish to do all in our power to worship and praise and celebrate the goodness of God is beyond dispute. That he created us primarily for those purposes is another claim altogether. The analogy with parenthood is illuminating here. A child rejoices to know that she has enhanced the joy or paternal pride or sense of well-being of her mother or father. To learn that she was conceived for that very purpose would be rather unsettling.

An illustration comes from the family life of Jonathan Edwards, known for his sermons about an angry God who held sinners over the pit of hell like loathsome spiders over a flame. On one occasion when Edwards was out of town, a local preacher named Peter Reynolds came to visit Edwards's wife, Sarah, and her children. He offered to have a prayer with the family, and she agreed. Perhaps, praying in the home of the famous preacher of fire and brimstone, Reynolds entreated God in tones he thought Edwards might have approved of. In any event, Sarah was troubled. She recorded in her journal that while the reverend was offering his prayer, she found herself feeling "an earnest desire that, in calling on God, he should say Father." Then she asked herself, "Can I . . . with the confidence of a child, and without the least misgiving of heart, call God my Father?" Pondering led to yearning. She "felt a strong desire to be alone with God" and withdrew to her chamber. In the moments that followed, "the presence of God was so near, and so real, that I seemed scarcely conscious of any thing else. God the Father, and the Lord Jesus Christ, seemed as distinct persons, both manifesting their inconceivable loveliness, and mildness, and gentleness, and their great and immutable love to me. . . . The peace and happiness, which I hereupon felt, was altogether inexpressible."[18]

Sarah Edwards, we now know, was correct. Her insight was inspired. But her experience of the Father's approachability was in spite of, not because of, the portrait of God that terrified thousands. How many millions then—and continuing to the present—yearn for a reassuring contact with, intimacy with, and accepting embrace by a Heavenly Parent? One inspired minister, Edward Beecher, wrote that "of all errors, none are so fundamental and so wide-reaching in their evil tendencies and results as errors with respect to the character of God."[19] Notice how similar this is to the prophet Joseph's words that a precondition for the exercise of an efficacious faith is a true knowledge of God's character and attributes.[20]

And here Restoration teachings break dramatically with the God of the creeds like the Westminster Confession. In the Bible, Job asks in wonder, "What is man . . . that thou shouldest set thine heart upon him?"[21] The astonishing fact that Joseph reveals is that God does set his heart upon us. To invest one's absolute love, of course, is to make oneself fully vulnerable. Parents as well as lovers have long learned this to their cost. We are never so defenseless, remarked Freud, as when we love.[22] Yet God *chooses* to love *us*. And if love means responsibility, sacrifice, vulnerability, then God's decision to love us is the most stupendously sublime moment in the history of time. It is God's response to the manifold creatures by whom he is surrounded, the movement of his heart and will in the direction of those other beings—us— that becomes the defining moment in his godliness and establishes the pattern of his divine activity. His freely made choice to inaugurate and sustain costly loving relationships is the very core of his divine identity.

We find the most sublime scriptural evidence of this in Joseph's revelation of the Book of Moses. The prophet Enoch is taken into heaven and records his ensuing vision. He sees Satan's dominion over the earth and God's unanticipated response to a world veiled in darkness: "The God of heaven looked upon the residue of the people, and He wept; and Enoch bore record of it, saying: How is it that the heavens weep, and shed forth their tears as the rain upon the mountains? And Enoch said unto the Lord: How is it that thou canst weep?" The question here is not about the reasons behind God's tears. Enoch does not ask, why do you weep, but rather, how are your tears even possible, "seeing thou art holy, and from all eternity to all eternity?" Clearly, Enoch, who believed God to be "merciful and kind forever," did not expect such a being could be moved to the point of distress by the sins of his children. And so a third time he asks, "How is it thou canst weep?" The answer, it turns out, is that God is not exempt from emotional pain. Exempt? On the contrary, God's pain is as infinite as his love. He weeps because he feels compassion. As the Lord explains to Enoch,

> Unto thy brethren have I said, and also given commandment, that they should love one another, and that they should choose me, their Father; but behold, they are without affection, and they hate their own blood . . . and misery shall be their doom; and the whole heavens shall weep over them, even all the workmanship of mine hands; wherefore should not the heavens weep, seeing these shall suffer?[23]

It is not their wickedness but their "misery," not their disobedience but their "suffering" that elicits the God of heaven's tears. Not until Gethsemane and Golgotha does the scriptural record reveal so unflinchingly the costly investment of God's love for his people, the price at which he placed his heart upon them.

The question that should now appear on the faith horizon is "why?" Why should a God of perfect holiness make himself vulnerable to the lives and choices and suffering of a human progeny? Why did he create us or—in Joseph Smith's original conception—adopt us as his children? The Book of Moses tells us in emphatic, explicit terms that our creation was not calculated for God's own benefit but for ours. Against the long record rehearsed above of God's desire for his own glory, Moses 1:39 assumes the shocking power of inspired novelty: "My work and my glory is to bring about [*your*] immortality and eternal life," not God's own glory. Or as Lehi teaches, "Men are, that *they* might have joy."[24] Joseph Smith affirmed, "What was the purpose of the almighty in making man? It was to exalt *him* to be as God" (my emphases).[25] This is a conception of God that may well come closer than any other in religious history to a literalizing of God's role and status as divine parent, not a sovereign.

There is beauty and power in knowing we have Heavenly Parents who are actually, truly invested in our happiness and in our sorrows. And there is a transformative freedom in recognizing that God has made our eternal happiness their personal project. ("*Their* goal, *their* work, and *their* glory," said Elder Theodore M. Burton (my emphasis).[26]) We find ourselves participating in a divine solidarity, trusting that our happiness becomes their own, as do our burdens of sadness. They do not remove themselves from the human drama so as to render their eternal peace and joy immune to our struggles.

If you do not realize the radical novelty of such a conception of God, it may be a result of the fact that in the decades after Joseph Smith's revelation of Enoch's encounter with the weeping God of heaven, there began to be a paradigm shift in the Christian community. The scholar Thomas Weinandy observed in *First Things* that "toward the end of the nineteenth century a sea change began to occur within Christian theology such that at present many, if not most, Christian theologians hold as axiomatic that God is passible, that He does undergo emotional changes of states, and so can suffer."[27] Happily, a growing number of theologians have embraced the nature of the weeping God restored by Joseph Smith. Nicholas Wolterstorff, for example, writes that "God is not only the God of the sufferers but the God who suffers. . . . Instead of explaining our suffering God shares it."[28]

Ronald Goetz has referred to the surge in "theopaschism" (the affirmation of a suffering God) as a "revolution," marking a "structural shift in the Christian mind." He opines, "We have only begun to see where systematic theologies grounded in the suffering God might lead."[29] Paul L. Gavrilyuk states that there is now "a remarkable consensus" behind the claim that "God suffers."[30] Check any Christian bookstore for shelves with titles such as *Most Moved Mover*, *The God Who Risks*, and *The Suffering of God*. Latter-day Saint heresy, in other words, became mainstream Christian thought by the century's end.

After I made a public presentation to this effect at a Protestant seminary, the dean of the College of Theology protested that his faith tradition had long taught the same truths. I asked him how he reconciled that claim with his tradition's creeds. He paused a moment, then replied, "We don't really pay much attention to those." One beauty of the Restoration is that it concretized and canonized so many of those plain and precious truths that, in their radical resonance, have been intuited by multitudes of seekers open to the divine light. It is a rare treasure to have not just hopeful speculation on the subject but sacred scripture revealed in the Restoration's infancy.

PREEXISTENCE

The same Restoration text that revealed the extent of God's profoundly felt empathy contained the first unmistakable basis for a specifically human preexistence, leading to both poetic celebration and theological development of the theme. In Joseph Smith's account, Enoch learns in a vision about "the spirits that God had created . . . not visible to the natural eye" and is told clearly and unambiguously, "I am God; I made the world, and men before they were in the flesh."[31] So why is this idea important, and how does it serve as another door of faith? What theological and philosophical richness flows from this simple idea? And how may its recognition help to assuage the wounded condition of the human family?

We may begin by asking how far back in history a belief in our premortal existence goes. All the way to the beginning.[32] Varieties of premortality exist in the oldest creation narratives, like the Mesopotamian story "Atra-Hasis." Plato explicated the belief in several of his dialogues, most famously in *Meno*.[33] He used logic, analogy, and deduction to make his point. In the *Symposium*, he relied upon the simple human experience of falling in love. Human love, he was convinced, was an imperfect echo of prior knowledge of a more perfect beauty. At some earlier time, he believed, "Beauty was radiant to see at that time when the souls, along with the glorious chorus, . . . saw that blessed and spectacular vision. . . . Now beauty, as I said, was radiant among the other objects; and now that we have come down here we grasp it sparkling through the clearest of our senses." It can only be so experienced by someone "who has seen much in heaven."[34] But how do we know that mortal love is not the real thing? Because, as he writes elsewhere, we spend our lives searching for someone to make us complete. And when two such lovers find each other, he writes, "The two are struck from their senses by love, by a sense of belonging to one another, and by desire, and they don't want to be separated from one another, not even for a moment. These are the people who finish out their lives together." And yet, Plato concludes, as Augustine will later, a haunting lack persists. "It's obvious that the soul of every lover longs for something else; his soul cannot say what it is, but like an oracle it has a sense of what it wants, and like an oracle it hides behind a riddle."[35] For Augustine, our intimations are more definite. We seek for a happiness we intuit, he argued. And like the woman in the parable looking for a lost coin, we cannot seek something we have not already known.[36]

Talmudic sources assign the angel Gabriel the task of bringing spirits to the place appointed to enter their bodies. You might not remember that moment in your own past, but your body bears the imprint of those last moments in the spirit world. Just locate the gentle cleft in your upper lip, the philtrum. Here is a Hasidic account of where it comes from:

> When a baby is conceived an angel accompanies the soul into the womb. And in the blood-thumping shelter of the mother, angel and soul speak of the life to come and decide together on the purpose of this incarnation. What is this soul coming to contribute? Who will help support this purpose? What challenges will be faced? Where comes love? There is, of course, a catch to all this thoughtful planning. Just as the birth pangs begin, when the soul must fully enter the baby-self and the angel return to heaven, the angel reaches out and presses its finger against the baby's lip. We still have this mark, an indentation that runs sweetly from upper lip to nose. The philtrum is the angel's last gift. "Hush" it whispers to the stirring child, "now you must forget."[37]

From Mesopotamian and classical sources alike, belief in the preexistence made its way into the early Christian church. Origen was its principal proponent. Many of his teachings resonate with Latter-day Saint doctrines. This early third-century figure clearly taught of the Godhead in ways that resonate with our understanding. God and Jesus Christ exist as "two persons," he wrote, "one in unity of thought, in harmony . . . of will."[38] He believed in the same capacious heaven as Joseph Smith, convinced that God would find a way to redeem and exalt all his spirit children. (In his words, "gradually, and by degrees, during the lapse of infinite and immeasurable ages, . . . improvement and correction will be realized."[39]) He was reputed to teach that spirit is a higher form of matter,[40] and he taught that "the Father, too, himself, the God of the universe, 'patient and abounding in mercy' and compassionate, does He not in some way suffer? Or do you not know that when He directs human affairs, He suffers human suffering?"[41] No God devoid of body, parts, and passions for Origen. Finally, this church father agreed that the Fall was necessary and educative, not tragic and misguided: "You could not have reached the palm-groves unless you had experienced the harsh trials; you could not have reached the gentle springs without first having to overcome sadness and difficulties."[42] Tragically, over the centuries, each and every one of these inspired teachings of Origen was explicitly anathematized or exiled from the orthodox faith. This happened even though Origen was indisputably "the greatest theologian the Eastern Church has produced" by one reckoning;[43] "the most learned and able divine of the ante-Nicene period, the Plato . . . of the Greek church," according to Philip Schaff;[44] and second only to Paul, according to another scholar.[45]

Origen was most remembered for his teaching that we mortals all enjoyed a life in heaven before birth. Though he differed in some particulars from Restoration conceptions, he believed that we were sentient beings, exercised our will in various ways, and were embodied in a school for moral improvement. An origin in the heavens, he further taught, portended a universal destiny there.

Once again in this story of lost truth, we should find inspiration in the resilience of an idea that continued to find expression through inspired outliers of orthodoxy, waiting only for Joseph Smith to elaborate the teaching. In the seventeenth century, a group of churchmen known as the Cambridge Platonists would answer Tertullian's query. Why should it be surprising, they reasoned, if the soul cannot recall all that has passed when, in the brief span of life, we have again forgotten so much? For "who can call to mind / Where first he here saw sunne or felt the gentle wind?"[46] Henry More, the most prolific member of this group, was sure there was proof of preexistence in those traces that clearly do remain. "The Idea of a Being absolutely and fully Perfect . . . is Naturall and Essentiall to the Soul of Man, & cannot be washt out, nor conveigh'd away by any force or trick."[47] He wrote thousands of lines of poetry elaborating a doctrine of preexistence as the most plausible explanation for this phenomenon, such as these lines:

> I would sing the pre-existency
> Of human souls and live once o'er again
> By recollection and quick memory
> All that is passed since first we all began.
> But all too shallow be my wits to scan
> So deep a point.[48]

A kindred spirit in this regard was Benjamin Whichcote, who noted that "no sooner doth the Truth of God come to our soul's sight, but our soul knows her, as her first and old Acquaintance."[49] Another of that group, Nathanael Culverwell, in trying to account for human recognition of core truths, similarly refers to "seeds of light . . . scatter'd in the Soul of Man . . . which fill it with a vigorous pregnancy, with a multiplying fruitfulnesse, so that it brings forth a numerous and sparkling posterity."[50] When the eye of the soul looks upon God, he writes, it apprehends "those beamings out of eternal and universal Notions, that flow from him, as the Fountain of Lights, where they have dwelt from everlasting," and he refers to the life we live as a descent, a coming "down from the Mount" and putting on "the veil of Sense."[51]

Other thinkers from Descartes through the nineteenth century commonly invoked preexistence to explain the innate sense of universals, of morality, and of God. Echoing the Cambridge writers, the philosopher Immanuel Kant confessed that "two things fill [me with wonder]: the starry heavens above me and the moral law within me."[52] Whence could we have acquired that moral faculty which intuition told him was not a simple social or cultural acquisition? Kant would eventually come round to preexistence from three separate arguments. His most unphilosophical sounding argument is based entirely on the human sense of self—not logical, not empirical, but irrefutable. Kant asks whether it makes sense to believe that a being invested with an infinite potential, an eternal future, and a divine nature can be supposed to just spring into existence through casual sex or happenstance: "It is difficult to believe in the eternal existence of a being whose life has first begun under circumstances so trivial. . . . If we could see ourselves and other objects as they really are, we should see ourselves in a world of spiritual natures, which did neither begin at our birth nor will end with the death of the body."[53]

The question for us is, how does this restored truth of the soul's premortal existence open our eyes to new vistas, realities, and possibilities otherwise lost to us? Like many other philosophers and theologians of the nineteenth century, Kant saw in preexistence the only solution to the mystery of human free will. Influential German theologians of the era, such as Julius Müller, agreed: One must "look beyond the region of the temporal in order to find the original source of our freedom. . . . In this region we must seek that power of original choice." The alternative would make of us fully determined beings, incapable of sin or virtue.[54] As twentieth-century philosopher John McTaggart put the problem, if God created our spirits, he would be responsible for all our sins, for he could have created us with better natures. Only a self-existent intelligence, McTaggart (like Aristotle, Kant, and others) was arguing, would be a creature whose disposition and tendencies and character were not arbitrarily shaped by a Creator. Hence, he found the preexistence of the soul the only reasonable ground for both human freedom and human accountability.[55] If, as Joseph Smith taught, at the core of our identity, we are eternal, self-existent beings, then we are truly and unqualifiedly free and responsible agents.

These philosophical intimations evoke not just the reality of a realm of eternal truth behind the shadowy idols of the present but a realm that beckons to us through faint traces of memory that pierce the long night of forgetfulness. The novelist and essayist Marilynne Robinson has referred to the "odd privilege of existence as a coherent self, . . . that haunting *I* who wakes us in the night wondering where time has gone, the I we waken to, sharply aware that we have been unfaithful to ourselves."[56] We all know the sensation of having failed to live up to who we are—the sense that there exists a different "I" than the one sometimes manifest through our actions. This perception is ingrained in our very language of self-justification. "I wasn't myself," we might say. Or "you are better than that," a friend or relative might tell us after a disappointing course of conduct. Who is this "I" we are referring to in such instances? It could be just an idealized self we have failed to manifest, except that the sense is too strong that it is our actions that are unreal or fall short of an actual standard that already exists in some form. In other words, is our most plausible candidate a hypothetical self we might someday be? Or is it what George MacDonald called an "old soul,"[57] a self with a long history that provides the contrast between present patterns of behavior?

The French novelist Marcel Proust expressed similar stirrings of recognition, adding the element of covenants faintly remembered:

> All that we can say is that everything is arranged in this life as though we entered it carrying the burden of obligations contracted in a former life; there is no reason inherent in the conditions of life on this earth that can make us consider ourselves obliged to do good, to be fastidious, to be polite even, nor make the talented artist consider himself obliged to begin over again a score of times a piece of work the admiration aroused by which will matter little to his body devoured by worms. . . . All these obligations which have not their sanction in our present life seem to belong to a different world, founded upon kindness, scrupulosity, self-sacrifice, a world

entirely different from this, which we leave in order to be born into this world, before perhaps returning to the other to live once again beneath the sway of those unknown laws which we have obeyed because we bore their precepts in our hearts.[58]

Of this passage, philosopher Gabriel Marcel writes, "We are probably at first tempted to refer back to the Platonic myth which underlies this. There is, however, every reason to think that we should be making a serious mistake if we put the accent here on the word 'myth.'"[59]

One of the earliest church fathers, Clement of Alexandria who lived in the second century, felt the truth later intuited by Proust could explain the remarkable decision of an individual to abruptly reverse the course of one's life in quest of a better. This, he reasoned, can only be because when we sin, we sense we are falling short of who we really are. And he believed only memory of the past, not imagination about the future, could be a credible prompt to such repentance. In the midst of lowly actions, our souls sometimes resonate with the dim intimations of a heavenly past and evidence of a more supernal destiny than the one our poor choices foreshadow. As Clement wrote, we at some point come to a vague "reminiscence of better things" and desire to "renounce[e] our iniquities" and "speed back to the eternal light, children to the Father."[60]

By the sixth century, the institutional church consigned all such views as I have reviewed to the religious ash heap of heresy and put the doctrine's promoters and teachers under anathema. Inspired mystics, philosophers, and poets kept the idea alive, as we have seen. It was for the Prophet Joseph to restore to Christian understanding one of the most resilient and most significant keys to self-understanding.

Most transformatively, perhaps, Joseph's restoration of the truth about our identity and our participation in premortal councils tells us this important fact: We are not helpless victims of fate, cast ignominiously upon the shores of a hostile world. We participated in those decisions that led to this very earth's creation. We counted the costs of a hazardous and harrowing venture here, we gave our assent, and we did so for one reason. Robert Frost, in his most inspired poem, captured the setting. He described that scene, in premortal fields, when "very beautifully God limn[ed], and tenderly, life's little dream," and we, in response, "gladly gave up paradise . . . for some good [we] discerned"[61] because we trusted that our Heavenly Parents would shepherd us home again to a richer and more abundant life than we could otherwise know. We are collaborators, long-time pupils working under conditions and covenants in which we actively and knowingly—wittingly—participated. Dorothy Sayers was probably not familiar with this doctrine of our premortal life, but she well described its most empowering and enlightening implication: "The perfect work of love demands the co-operation of the creature." In this relationship with the divine, we find the perfect

> WE ARE NOT HELPLESS VICTIMS OF FATE, CAST IGNOMINIOUSLY UPON THE SHORES OF A HOSTILE WORLD. WE PARTICIPATED IN THOSE DECISIONS THAT LED TO THIS VERY EARTH'S CREATION.

synthesis of "the complete independence of the creature combined with its willing co-operation in [God's] purposes."[62] As Brigham Young urged, I hope that you might "cling to the principles of life that open eternity and reveal to us what we are, making known to us our relationship to God, which to the world is a great mystery."[63]

CHAPTER 3

Awful
Woundedness

*The other disciples said unto [Thomas], We have seen
the Lord. But he said unto them, Except I shall see in
his hands the print of the nails, and put my finger into
the print of the nails, and thrust my hand into his side,
I will not believe. And after eight days again his disciples were within, and Thomas with them: then came
Jesus, the doors being shut, and stood in the midst,
and said, Peace be unto you. Then saith he to Thomas,
Reach hither thy finger, and behold my hands; and
reach hither thy hand, and thrust it into my side: and
be not faithless, but believing. And Thomas answered
and said unto him, My Lord and my God.*[1]

WOUNDEDNESS

How do we come to know Christ? How do we recognize him—his presence in the world? Thomas came to know
of the persisting reality of Jesus Christ, his lived presence
in the world, when he actually felt his wounds. There is a

logical symmetry there. We only know Christ—really know him—to the extent that we know what his love for us cost him. And so, perhaps, that is the primary mode by which Christ knows and engages us—by our wounds. By feeling our wounds. That would seem to be the meaning of his words, "I have graven thee upon the palms of my hands."[2] We know him by his wounds as he knows us by ours.

We—in the West especially—live in an age of the technologically miraculous. Vaccines prevent illness, fluoride prevents cavities, anesthesia prevents pain, sunscreen prevents burns, and antioxidants are touted to prevent aging. But it is a fragile veneer, this array of safety nets. Even so, we pursue our dreams of protection. Disease, suffering, and death itself are viewed as failures of the system, the doctors, or the human organism itself. Life in fact seems stacked against us in a universe so utterly asymmetrical. It is so much easier to disrupt our well-being than it is to cement it. And an overwhelming preponderance of favorable variables is necessary for even a modicum of happiness. No one would comment cheerfully that all of their bones except three are unbroken, only one of their children is deathly sick, or only seven of their clients are suing them this week, so all in all, life is good. We are fragile beings in a precarious existence, vulnerable to the vicissitudes of natural laws and human agency with tragedy always hovering at the margins.

For centuries, humans took a doubtful consolation in accepting mortality's "slings and arrows" as the price to be paid for the fateful decisions made in Eden. An entirely typical traditional Christian account of the fall of Adam relates that "the story immediately unfolds with a catastrophe. . . . Evil follows evil . . . like an avalanche."[3] As a consequence, wrote Augustine (an influential bishop and a principal founder of creedal Christianity), humanity became "one mass of sin."[4] By the time of Joseph Smith, such rationalization for the human condition was losing its hold on the Christian imagination. A year after the First Vision, the poet Lord Byron spoke for growing numbers through the voice of his indignant character, Cain. Learning the reasons behind human—and personal—misery, he protests

> Life?—Toil! and wherefore should I toil?—because
> My father could not keep his place in Eden?
> What had *I* done in this?—I was unborn:
> I sought not to be born.[5]

However, no revised Christian narrative took shape to recast the origins of the human predicament or to return it to an explanation known to early Christians such as Irenaeus, who wrote of Eve and Adam's choice in Eden:

Wherefore [they have] also had a two-fold experience, possessing knowledge of both kinds, that with discipline [they] may make choice of the better things. But how, if he had no knowledge of the contrary, could he have had instruction in that which is good? . . . For just as the tongue receives experience of the sweet and bitter by means of tasting, . . . so also does the mind, receiving through the experience of both the knowledge of what is good, become more tenacious of its preservation by acting in obedience to God.[6]

It was for Latter-day Saint women of the nineteenth century to first realize how drastically the Restoration rewrote the founding narrative of Western civilization. In this new version, life is an educative ascent, not a catastrophic fall. And Christ is our healer from woundedness, not our rescuer from depravity. One of the first women with the great insight to challenge that view was the Latter-day Saint Relief Society President Sarah Kimball, who wrote in 1874, "Our great maternal progenitor is entitled to reverent honor for braving the peril that brought earth's children from the dark valley of ignorance and stagnation, and placed them on the broad, progressive plain, where they, knowing good and evil, joy and sorrow, may become as Gods. . . . Mother Eve, for taking the initiative in this advance movement, should receive encomiums of praise."[7] That is the upside of Latter-day Saint theology: The Fall was no fall but ascent. The human family is ushered into life by the courageous choice of Eve the heroine, not by the wicked weakness of Eve the sinner. Life is an upper division course in gradual sanctification, not a purgatory of inherited sin. And we Latter-day Saints are optimists. God, said Joseph Smith, will ferret out every soul that can be saved.[8] We believe in a God who wants peers, not subjects, and we have confidence that they—God jointly—will bring us to where they are.

The other side of the coin,

> THE HUMAN FAMILY IS USHERED INTO LIFE BY THE COURAGEOUS CHOICE OF EVE THE HEROINE, NOT BY THE WICKED WEAKNESS OF EVE THE SINNER.

however, is that our optimistic Latter-day Saint culture has at times made the path there look misleadingly easy. Our faith tradition aspires to make us into God's own likeness, divine beings in our own right, and then unite us in an endless community of the sanctified. Our sin, as Saints, may be in thinking such an endeavor could be anything other than wrenching, costly, inconceivably difficult, and unimaginably painful. We do not become, in C. S. Lewis's phrase, "little Christs" by a couple of well-spent hours ministering to our families and abstaining from tea and coffee. If we remember this principle, it can reshape our understanding of just what the purpose of the Church—its principles and institutional forms—is. And it turns out, this purpose may be close to the opposite of what we had thought. Brigham Young delivered perhaps the best sermon ever given to shake us out of misleading paradigms in this regard. "The gospel," he said,

> causes men and women to reveal that which would have slept in their dispositions until they dropped into their graves. The plan by which the Lord leads this people makes them reveal their thoughts and intents and brings out every train of disposition lurking in their [beings]. . . . Every fault that a person has will be made manifest, that it may be corrected by the gospel of salvation, by the laws of the Holy Priesthood.[9]

In this account, the point of the gospel may require our situatedness in a perpetual state of disequilibrium. These circumstances force to the surface every human flaw that our biology, our environment, and our own spiritual immaturity bring in their wake. That is the design behind the project. Evolution—in spiritual things as well as in biological organisms—is powered by tension, contestation, friction. These are the only conditions under which such sanctifying can take place. Contemporary research in the social sciences bears unexpected witness to this fact. A few years ago, Malcolm Gladwell popularized the 10,000-hour principle. Play chess for 10,000 hours, and you will be a grandmaster. Play music in European dives for 10,000 hours, and you can be the next Beatles. So will 10,000 hours of practice make you a saint? David Epstein wrote a brilliant corrective to Gladwell's book, called *Range*. Several of his findings may have eternal significance.

Epstein divides the world into two kinds of domains, called kind and wicked. A kind domain is one in which the rules are clear, the variables limited, the scenarios all fairly predictable, like playing tennis, golf, chess, or guitar. He notes that "pretending the world is like golf and chess is comforting. It makes for a tidy kind-world message, and some very compelling books."[10] But the other domain is what he calls a "wicked" domain (in the sense of devilishly challenging, not evil). "In wicked domains," he writes, "the rules of the game are often unclear or incomplete, there may or may not be repetitive patterns and they may not be obvious, and feedback is often delayed, inaccurate, or both."[11] And here's his bottom line: "When we know the rules and answers, and they don't change over time—chess, golf, playing classical music," we fall into the trap that he calls "cognitive entrenchment."[12]

Those who expose themselves to "wicked domains," by contrast, become what he calls "successful adapters." "They dr[a]w on outside experiences and analogies to interrupt their inclination toward a previous solution that may no longer work."[13] Much of his book is an advertisement for wicked domains—range, breadth, challenging environments, diversity of experience, and education—as the key to flourishing. But I want to zero in on the relevance of these two principles of cognitive entrenchment and successful adaptation in particular. Because with these two terms, we find a powerful vocabulary for why some Saints flourish in the midst of life's challenges, while others "dwindle in unbelief."[14] These are the only two options before you. These were the only two options open to Adam and Eve.

You find a place of comfort and security, and you stay there—safe but in stasis, happy but fragile. Or you make the choice to enter a fraught field of dissonance and uncertainty, and you adapt creatively as you go along. This applies with special force to faith and testimony. A testimony is a paradigm. You have a comprehensive schema for making sense of life. It consists of a set of principles, rules, and expectations. They include your deeply held beliefs about the nature of revelation, the role and character of prophets, the reliability of scripture, and what it means to call a church "true" or to "know" God lives. And then, a few steps outside the Garden, catastrophe strikes. Revelation fails you. Prophets err. Scripture manifests inconsistencies. The institution shows its flaws, and God is silent in the face of human tragedy.

What do you do? Eighty years ago, the moral philosopher A. D. Lindsay said this about true disciples. They see

> the situation and say, "Here is a mess, a crying evil, a need! What can you do about it?" We are asked

not to say "Yes" or "No" or "I will" or "I will not,"
but to be inventive, to create, to discover something
new. The difference between ordinary people and
saints is not that saints fulfill the plain duties which
ordinary men neglect. The things saints do have not
usually occurred to ordinary people at all. . . . [This
process] is like the work of the artist. It needs imagination and spontaneity. It is not a choice between
presented alternatives but the creation of something new.[15]

The creation of something new. I love and admire the
vision of Lindsay because he sees the life of faith, of discipleship, as a moral and intellectual adventure. We must
embrace the challenge of a life of strenuous spiritual endeavor. Fear makes us timid, but the doctrine of the Restoration is nothing if not a challenge to resist the lethargy
and inertia that are the perennial temptation of the doubtful. The Latter-day Saint poet John Harris, in an essay ti-
tled "Risk and Terror," notes that "the function of parents,
like the function of teachers, is to work themselves out of a
job." He then takes the radical but logical step of propos-
ing that "even God's job—is essentially one of weaning."[16]
Such an idea is unorthodox to say the least, but Brigham
Young taught it explicitly. God's own purposes envision the
gradual emancipation of human pupils from divine depen-
dence. "They are organized to be just as independent as any
being in eternity. . . . [We are] calculated to be as independent as the Gods, in the end. . . . [But] I do not expect to
see the day when I am perfectly independent, until I am
crowned in the celestial kingdom of my Father, and made as

independent as my Father in heaven." "This is the place where every man commences to acquire the germ of the independence that is enjoyed in the heavens," he said on another occasion.[17]

Observers have admired this bracing vision of Restoration theology, even if we have sometimes forgotten it. "The Mormon emphasis is upon action," noted the Catholic sociologist Thomas O'Dea, upon "the vigorous exercise of the will," and even "God's supreme position is understood not in terms of his being a First Necessary Being but rather as a result of a 'conquest.'"[18] The courage to act with the imagination and creativity of Lindsay's ideal disciple would flow more naturally if we embraced the vision of God that Joseph imparted. The most underrated lesson he learned in his First Vision was that God, indeed, does not "upbraid" us in our tentative groping for understanding. We might indeed "venture" forth in spite of misgivings and apprehensions.[19] Joseph taught that it is in knowing how "merciful and gracious . . . and full of goodness" our God is that we can find the antidote to the fear that paralyzes us, the terror of thinking or believing wrongly.[20]

Consequently, it is not to be wondered at that a testimony—the paradigm by which you live your life and decipher its meaning—must be continually rebuilt with every new morning. Some have criticized testimony adjustment as mental gymnastics. Is reconstituting a paradigm—or a testimony—in the light of new information a virtuoso performance of intellectual agility? Of course it is. We must engage in perpetual mental calisthenics too because the alternative is mental timidity and sloth—cognitive entrenchment. Our paths to discipleship, in other words, must be individuated. They should be the product of a strenuously achieved personal understanding, not an effortless embrace of a template.

We would do well to adopt the attitude of the great Catholic cardinal John Henry Newman, who said, "Ten thousand difficulties do not add up to a doubt,"[21] or of the great Anglican theologian Austin Farrer, who wrote, "I shall not call my faith in doubt, for since God has shown to me a ray of his goodness, I cannot doubt him on the ground that someone has made up some new logical puzzles about him. It is too late in the day to tell me that God does not exist, the God with whom I have so long conversed, and whom I have seen active in several men [and women] of real sanctity."[22]

David Bentley Hart is something of an iconoclast. He has been called the preeminent theologian of our day. He makes this unsettling claim about the New Testament: "In a sense, the good news announced by scripture was that Christ had come to save humanity from the burden of Christianity."[23] Christ saves us from the burden of Christianity? To what burden of Christianity is Hart referring? And do we find similar burdens in the Church of Jesus Christ? If we turn to the first crisis in the primitive Church, we find the early controversies in the Church in Palestine were rooted in this very dilemma: What practices were authentically Christian? And which elements were simply cultural inheritance, assumptions, and expectations—i.e., burdens—externally imposed? In the book of Acts, we read of a "great dissension" that broke out on this question as that small Galilean sect first began its long progress to becoming a global religion. "You are not Christians 'after the manner of Moses,'" some of the old crowd protested, regarding foreign converts with deep-seated suspicion as they were not observers of Jewish law; Peter's admonition to his fellow apostles and elders still rings with relevance today: "Now therefore why . . . put a yoke upon the neck of the disciples, which neither our fathers nor we were able to bear?"[24]

As Brigham Young declaimed, "Away with stereotyped Mormons!"[25] Don't let the expectations of others become a yoke on your neck. Internalize and authenticate your religious commitments. We might fruitfully adapt Hart's provocation to our predicament. If we read Mark's manual of discipleship, also called his Gospel, we find a recurrent theme. Note how it unfolds: The first verses are set in the wilderness. The first chapter ends "in the desert places." In chapter 6, he tells his apostles, "Come ye yourselves apart into a desert place."[26] When he heals one who is deaf, a chapter later, "he took him aside from the multitude."[27] In chapter 8, the crowd "[brought] a blind man unto him. . . And he took the blind man by the hand, and led him out of the town."[28] In a later episode, he takes Peter, James, and John "apart by themselves."[29] We serve and we worship in community. But we come closest to the Holy of Holies as individuals. In pursuing the life of discipleship, the point seems to be that of course the path to divinization is narrow and ultimately lonely. It only admits one, and that one is you. How do we fashion that path? Two constants in the quest stand out: our intellectual limitations and the interdependence of discipleship.

INTELLECTUAL LIMITATIONS

To open the doors of faith is to commit to a stance of radical epistemic humility. It is to begin with Nephi's frank acknowledgement: "I do not know the meaning of all things."[30] It is to embrace with blithe regard the indisputable reality that "there are more things in heaven and earth . . . than are dreamt of in your philosophy."[31] And it is to venture willingly outside the confines and safety of skepticism in order to make the fullest sense out of our wounded, human predicament.

We should welcome challenges to our faith as an opportunity to reshape our understanding of God, his nature, and his activity in the universe. Be as open to wonderment and teachability as Moses, who—confronted with a vision of the universe that totally annihilated his paradigm—was glad to learn things he "never had supposed";[32] be as adaptable as Joseph Smith, who learning a new truth about God's capacious heaven confessed that he "marveled" at what— and who—he saw there;[33] and be as open to other worlds as the prophet's servant, who with eyes now opened beheld "the mountain . . . was full of horses and chariots of fire round about Elisha."[34] Don't be cognitively entrenched as so many are when confronted with challenges like the Book of Abraham, a stumbling block to many in the faith because it disrupts our expectations of how the revelatory process should work. Only now are our own institutional histories coming to grapple with the complexities of these prophetic processes. Consider the apostle Paul who, having a visionary experience, was unsure of what he was even experiencing: "Whether in the body, I cannot tell; or whether out of the body, I cannot tell."[35] His confession is telling.

For those open to the divine voice, God speaks through manifold means, which often surprise and confound us. Maybe he speaks through the voice of another or in the still small voice only you may hear. Perhaps you hear by way of those "holy men [and women]" that Joseph "kn[e]w not of": poets, priests, and saints of other faiths.[36] Waking visions and dreams in the night speak to some. Scriptures unfold themselves to us as we liken them to ourselves, and a prophet's words may pierce our heart as if heaven sent and aimed. Seekers may find themselves visited in a sacred grove, like Adam in the Garden, or they may pursue understanding through study, prayer, and linguistic application.

Despite his efforts, Joseph Smith could not create a grammar of Egyptian, but his efforts to do so are nothing if not impressive. At the end of his years of wrestling to decipher ancient manuscripts, he produced a text through means he may not himself have fully understood, any more than Paul's anonymous visionary. This is a deal breaker for some in the faith community. That is, to my mind, unfortunate. God dwells in "everlasting burnings";[37] Job's presumption to fit God's behavior into tidy predictable categories was personally catastrophic, and Moses was left to marvel at his finitude before the infinitude of the cosmos and its Creator. The abstractions and paradoxes of Trinitarian thought may have made God too remote and impersonal; however, in our embrace of the corporeal, parental God, an opposite danger lurks. We as Saints have perhaps diminished God's majesty by our glib familiarity and thought to tame and domesticate the blinding light into a pleasant, nonthreatening nightlight. I want to inhabit a tradition where the novel, the unexpected, and the indecipherable can still irrupt. And I cannot help but admire Joseph Smith's insatiable appetite in his attempt to penetrate the veils of heaven and of history, the intellectual and spiritual energies with which he pursued his task, and his indifference to the uneven results of his own ongoing and ever incomplete explorations.

We want our religious narratives to be simple and straightforward. But God's workings invariably disappoint such expectations. There's an apt corollary in modern science. As physicists and cosmologists have probed both the wider cosmos and the subatomic realms, they find that reality defies familiar assumptions at every turn. Quantum theory, for example, reveals that nature at its most fundamental level is "absurd from the point of view of common sense."[38] Matter consists of waves unless you measure for particles. So it consists of particles unless you measure for waves. We don't really even know what matter is. As John Gribbin writes, "It will [appear as either a wave or particle] depending on what measurements we choose to carry out on it."[39] "In the world of the very small, . . . things do not behave in any way that we can understand from our experience of the everyday world . . . all pictures are false, and there is no physical analogy we can make to understand what goes on."[40] Gary Zukav makes such weirdness even stranger: "According to quantum physics," he writes, "a subatomic particle is not [really] a particle. . . . Rather, subatomic particles are 'tendencies to exist.' . . . They have no objective existence."[41]

As one science writer summarizes, physicists now reject three ideas about our universe that were until a few generations ago foundational and unchallenged: locality (the idea that an event in one place cannot simultaneously affect an event in another place), reality (the universe and its elements exist independently of observation or measurement), and determinism (the law of causality—all effects are determined by causes).[42] These three ideas, essential to any basic or intuitive understanding of the world, are now contested by virtually all physicists. New paradigms striving to make new sense of our world include string theory with its eleven dimensions and the multiverse, positing an infinite number of entire universes with infinite iterations of you. Hugh Everett III postulates famously that every time we make a measurement, the entire universe splits in twain. Both universes are now equally real, but we "are forced by the process of observation to select one of these alternatives, which becomes part of what we see as the 'real' world; the act of observation cuts the ties that bind alternative realities together, and allows them to go on their own separate ways."[43]

It gets worse (or better if you like Kafka). At a deeper level, there may be no such thing as place and no such thing as distance, suggests George Musser.[44] And quantum theorist Carlo Rovelli notes how "not only is there no single time for different places. . . . There is no special moment on [any other planet] that corresponds to what constitutes the here and now" for us. Simultaneity does not exist.[45] Newton's universe—once stable, coherent, and predictable—has become foreign, indecipherable, and saturated in mystery and paradox. As John Wheeler summarizes, all these problems involving the deeper reality behind appearances "are outside our usual language for talking about them."[46]

Since basics as seemingly simple as space and time and matter continue to thwart the greatest minds in the human race, it hardly seems reasonable to expect that our transactions with the divine should be more predictable and straightforward, fitting into neat categories and expectations. How naïve and presumptuous to insist that while our universe, in its deepest structure, is beyond our modes of either visualization or comprehension, God and his workings should not be. Yes, God may communicate at times in ways familiar and accessible, but we should not mistake such glimpses for the full picture of his absolute nature. Perhaps authentic encounters with the divine will always be disruptive of both our expectations and our paradigms.

The German Helmuth von Moltke famously wrote that "no battle plan survives contact with the enemy."[47] (Mike Tyson was a bit more earthy: "Everybody has a plan until they get punched in the face."[48]) Nor does a testimony forged without cost survive first contact with the forces of entropy and chaos that assault us outside the walls of Eden. That is the point. Only the suffering and skepticism and cognitive dissonance we encounter in a fallen world can provide the fiery catalyst to propel us out of our cognitive entrenchment and force us to employ all our spiritual and intellectual resources to open our hearts and minds to a truth that eludes our perfect comprehension. To return again to Mark, in chapter 8, we witness a peculiar instance of healing a blind man, whom Christ has led out of the town. Jesus spits on his hands, places them on the man's face, and asks, do you see anything? To which an undoubtedly disappointed patient replies, "I see men as trees, walking." What are we to make of this? Has the great Physician and Healer failed? Jesus repeats the procedure, and this time, the healing takes. He "saw every man clearly."[49] Mark has just taught an important dimension about the path of discipleship. We see the full picture incrementally as our vision only gradually keeps pace with the great revelation. Even after the Master's first touch, the blind man saw imperfectly. But because he did not turn in disappointment from the Healer, his capacity to see grew measure by measure.

Mark is incredibly focused on a particular kind of humility, teachability, as a prerequisite for earnest discipleship. From his very first appearance in the synagogue to his final days, incomprehension and bewilderment follow the Christ. The crowds "were astounded," Mark says at one point; "Never before have we seen the like."[50] On another occasion, an audience was "astonished," asking, "Where does he get these things?"[51]

Strangers, of course, are entirely clueless. We expect that. Is he John the Baptist? Elias? Another prophet? It is easy to find the humor, the hint of smug superiority, in our own reaction. Poor, blind contemporaries, ignorant of who it was that walked among them. Mark's point is that his true disciples are almost equally clueless. Neither his family, his confidants, nor his disciples get him. "He is beside himself," they say in embarrassment at one point.[52] A while later, they say to one another incredulously, "What manner of man is this?"[53] In yet another episode, his disciples "were sore amazed in themselves beyond measure, and wondered."[54] Translators struggle to convey their utter incomprehension. These, his closest followers, were "utterly astounded"[55] and "exceedingly beyond measure amazed."[56] They were, in short, stupefied.

If those who walked with him, broke bread with him, and were personally tutored by Jesus were stupefied, amazed, dumbfounded, and perplexed, then I must expect to be filled with even more wonderment. If I am not, it is not because I comprehend more than they; it is because the story has been dulled in its retelling. Christ's effigy is worn by millions, his face omnipresent in art, his very title a label assumed by over a billion. He has become, in a word, deceptively familiar. Mark is trying to humble me. He says, in effect, "You need to wonder more and assume less. You need to break through all the familiar ways of seeing and hearing him and begin again."[57]

INTERDEPENDENCE OF DISCIPLESHIP

One other principle is essential in the faith journey—we must recognize the interdependence of discipleship. We cannot begin to fathom the nature of God or their purposes for us without recognizing the depth of their concern for the entire human family. Only to the extent that we grow to feel and demonstrate that same concern can we comprehend the source of all love and light. That seems to be a nonnegotiable fact about knowledge of divine things. The seventeenth-century preacher John Smith was right:

> That which enables us to know and understand aright the things of God must be a living principle of holiness within us. . . . Divine truth is better understood as it unfolds itself in the purity of men's hearts and lives, than in all those subtle niceties into which curious wits may lay it forth. . . . Some men have too bad hearts to have good heads. . . . He that will find truth must seek it with a free judgment and a sanctified mind.[58]

John Wesley's mother, Susanna, described a discipleship configured to make her son susceptible to those heavenly sources whence truth and wisdom originate: "Take this rule:

Whatever weakens your reason, impairs the tenderness of your conscience, obscures your sense of God, takes off the relish of spiritual things . . . that thing is sin to you, however innocent it may be in itself."[59] At the same time, that sanctification for which we strive can only follow from motives that are other-centered. Mother Teresa reminded us that "we must become holy, not because we want to feel holy, but because Christ must be able to live his life fully in us. We are to be all love, all faith, all purity, for the sake of the poor we serve."[60]

We are all interdependent in ways we don't even fathom—for starters because our very personhood remains incomplete and cannot flourish in solitary condition. When I was a child, year after year, I asked for an ant farm. And year after year, my parents complied. I anxiously ran outside, scooped up a cupful of ants from the desert's abundant ant hills, placed them in the plastic cubicle, and watched them slowly die. (This experience colored my perception of a tragic universe!) Ants can only function as a community. In isolation, remote from their community, they not only fail to thrive, they die. Psychologists and social workers know the cost of human isolation. (This is why one prominent neuroscientist writes that "solitary confinement in jail—enforced loneliness—is like capital punishment in slow motion."[61]) But the Restoration elevates social fact to theological principle. An exalted being is dual, consisting of two unified, sanctified individuals. Sanctification is a communal affair. There is no Zion individual. We are, as Aristophanes intuited, semi-beings apart from the condition of belonging.[62]

We may not realize how great are our powers to assist—

or to hinder—each other in our heavenward aspirations. One of the most astonishing things Joseph said about the celestial kingdom was that "if you do not accuse each other God will not accuse you. If you have no accuser you will enter heaven."[63] If you take him at his word, that is a terrifying specter. Not only must we forgive all offenders to participate in heaven but we must be forgiven by all those who have taken offense at our words or deeds—with good reason or not. That hardly seems fair, but it is based on a peculiarly Latter-day Saint version of heaven. Heaven is no less and no more than sanctified individuals thriving in sanctified relationality. Someone's refusal to forgive me impedes our relationship and—in that way—constrains my heaven as well as hers; worthiness is not the only criterion for celestial life. Through our choices, we construct or delimit the heaven that others will or will not enjoy.

> HEAVEN IS NO LESS AND NO MORE THAN SANCTIFIED INDIVIDUALS THRIVING IN SANCTIFIED RELATIONALITY.

This is why the words of the superb historical novelist, Dorothy Dunnett, have particular force for me:

Some live all their lives without discovering this truth; that the noblest and most terrible power we possess is the power we have, each of us, over the chance-met, the stranger, the passer-by outside your life and your kin. Speak . . . as you would write: as if your words were letters of lead, graven there for all time, for which you must take the consequences. *And take the consequences.*[64]

In the great novel *The Power and the Glory*, Graham Greene's wise but flawed priest experiences this same epiphany in his encounter with the "small, malicious child." Suddenly, "he was aware of an immense load of responsibility: it was indistinguishable from love."[65]

HEALING

The story of the blind man discussed above is suggestive of the other side of woundedness: What does it mean to see Jesus Christ as our Healer? How do we find access to this healing power? Thomas knew Christ by his wounds, as Christ knows us by ours. And we all have them. As the philosopher Nicholas Wolterstorff has written, "We all suffer. For we all prize and love; and in this present existence of ours, prizing and loving yield suffering. Love in our world is suffering love. Some do not suffer much, though, for they do not love much. Suffering is for the loving."[66]

We know that we can lift each other in our pain. But Christ cannot lift us out of ours if he is just a theological construct. Does theology matter? Yes, for the simple reason that a correct theology is more conducive to a vital faith than an incorrect theology. Irenaeus referred to Christianity as "the only true and life-giving faith."[67] We could read that phrase as a gloss on the scriptural version "only true church" because it emphasizes what our faith—if accurately articulated—is capable of *doing*. Let me give three examples of how theology matters—how it can prepare the ground for us to move from Christ as theological construct to Christ as life-giving and life-healing Physician. Let me preface them with an illustration taken from a contemporary study of human motivation and human trust. Matt Ridley describes experiments conducted with students employing the "prisoner's dilemma" game, "in which each player must decide whether to cooperate in the hope of a mutual gain or defect in the hope of a selfish gain." Here was one alarming fact drawn from the study: "Economics students, who have been taught the self-interested nature of human beings, are twice as likely to defect," breaking faith in the hopes of personal gain.[68]

Ridley's point is not a criticism of economics majors; rather, his point was that economics students are trained to expect self-interestedness as a fundamental human fact. The lesson of the experiment? What we believe to be true of our own deepest nature and what we believe to be true of God's nature has real world consequences. The finer points of our beliefs matter. Who we are, why we are here, what our destiny is, what factors are conducive to our fullest thriving, and what kind of Being presides over our lives—the form we give such conceptions has a profound and, in the example cited, measurable impact on the nature of our human interactions, our relationships, our capacity to engage meaningfully in the world's work of healing.

Three Restoration teachings are particularly life-giving. They are re-definitions of the Fall, sin, and atonement. First, as I indicated briefly at the outset, we tell a different story about the Garden. We do not believe human life began with a catastrophe or that humanity is a seething mass of sin. We have a different account, one which echoes that of Eastern fathers. In this version, "The inheritance of the Fall [is] an inheritance . . . of mortality rather than sinfulness, sinfulness being merely a consequence of mortality."[69] It is the collateral damage we experience—and inflict—in the course of learning to prize the good, the sweet. The Eden story may give us a fresh way to think about this. If eating the fruit was not the sin that Christianity reads into the story, then where did the first sin lie? Perhaps in those first actions the story depicts immediately following. Adam, fearing to take responsibility for his action, places the blame on Eve. Eve, hesitating to own her action, shifts fault to the serpent. We are wired for self-defense, for survival, for self-interest. Perhaps the real sin is not in those spontaneous errors of judgment, those surrenders to what is natural and primal. That is not where the genuine guilt falls. Perhaps the first sin, the original sin, is only in our refusal to fully acknowledge, to own, to concede our inevitable error, and embrace the task of change. We are afraid to relinquish our "inner heroic narrative" or frankly confess ourselves to be the weak and undeveloped spiritual children we are.[70] As the philosopher Charles Taylor so wisely wrote, if there is a key substrate to all sin, it is this: "Our resistance to going along with God's initiative in making suffering reparative."[71] Dorothy Sayers, as we saw, agrees, writing that "the perfect work of love demands the co-operation of the creature."[72] Sin was meant to be educative, not damning.

This suggests, in turn, a different conception of atonement. If we briefly trace the history of the word, we can learn what we have lost. Working in the fourteenth century, the Englishman John Wycliffe was determined that every boy at the plow should be able to read the Bible in his native tongue. In Romans chapter 5, he came to the culminating work of Jesus Christ's sacrifice, which he expressed in this language: "We glory in God by our Lord Jesus Christ, by whom we have received now reconciling."[73] The gift of Christ, in his language, is reconciliation to God, a coming to complete harmony and unity in love and forgiveness. This was the sum total of Jesus Christ's great work effected in Gethsemane and on the cross. It was a few centuries later that William Tyndale rendered Romans 5:11 this way: "We also joy in God by the means of our Lord Jesus Christ by whom we have received the at[-]one[-]ment."[74] But here is what we have lost: The word *at-one-ment* was cognate with another word that the great mystic Julian of Norwich had used a century earlier (and which I wish Tyndale had used). Seeing in vision the sacrifice of Jesus Christ, she wrote of her sorrow "to see that body in pain that is loved." In that shared suffering, she continued, "saw I a great oneing between Christ and us."[75]

In the broader Christian tradition, *atonement* came fairly quickly to signify the payment of a debt; suffering or pain undergone to rectify a past wrong; compensation or restitution. These ideas have become part of the theological heritage of a concept central to Christian understanding. However, it would be tragic if the mechanism by which atonement is carried out were to displace the effect it was meant to achieve. The Crucifixion was an event. The at-one-ing is still in process of fulfillment, hence the perennial injunctions in the Book of Mormon for us to reciprocate the gesture by ourselves moving to be "one'd"—or in Nephi's and Jacob's language, "reconciled"—to Christ.[76] Atonement does not describe something Christ did but something he hopes to achieve. Atonement should not serve primarily as a description of his heroic sacrifice but as a description of the product, the outcome, of that sacrifice. The term *atonement* is not a legal one, having reference to reparation or ransom or payment for sin, but as Julian's related term suggests, it is ontological—that is, it refers to a relationship that the sacrifice is meant to accomplish. As Julian imagines the words of Jesus, "I shall together gather you, and make you meek and mild, clean and holy, by oneing to me."[77] We have to do our part to bring the process to fruition by accepting, embracing, and redirecting our desires and affections and by performing the work of healing among all with whom we have influence.

Three facts suggest why our view of Christ can be enriched by adding the concept of Healer to that of Savior. First, as we saw earlier, Nephi learned that the primary condition of our mortal state is woundedness, not sinfulness. Second, in the New Testament, the Greek word *sozo* is employed to describe the act of healing, making whole, or making well. It is used in the stories of Jesus healing the blind, the lame, the possessed, the diseased, and even the dead. It is also used in Luke's story of the woman who anoints Jesus with her tears, the woman "which was a sinner."[78] To her, as to the blind, the lame, and the deceased, Jesus speaks the identical phrase: "Thy faith has [sesoken] thee." Yet in this instance, the King James translators render the verbal form of *sozo* not as she is "made whole" or "healed" as in the parallel cases; rather, she is assured that her faith has "saved" her. The phrase is translated, respectively: "thy faith hath made thee whole," "thy faith hath made thee whole," "thy faith hath saved thee."[79] This translation obscures one of the most important lessons the New Testament has to teach us: Sin is a form of spiritual wound, and it needs the Healer's touch as much as blindness, illness, or other infirmities. Christ tells the woman she is "healed" from her sin. That is why he concludes, "go in peace," "*free from the distress* experienced because of sin" as one translation renders Christ's words (my emphasis).[80] This single insight of Christ as Healer of all our "infirmities" could do more to reshape our conceptions of sin, worthiness, and Christ's role in our lives than almost any other principle lost in the ages before the Restoration.[81]

What an insight we have lost: divine forgiveness is a gesture of holy healing conducive of at-one-ment. I believe the clear textual evidence and Restoration scripture and pronouncements urge an addition to our conceptions about Christ's role in our lives. Saving and salvation are cold, impersonal, abstract ideas. In Christ's healing ministry, we see his personal touch, time and again. As Thomas felt the Christ's wounds, so did Christ feel those of the lame, the blind, the afflicted of every sort. So does he feel ours. If we are rooted in these restored truths about the purpose behind our mortal sojourn and the true nature and healing role of Jesus Christ, we can be more deeply motivated to accept Christ's invitation to be one with him and bring his work of at-one-ment to completion.

> IN CHRIST'S HEALING MINISTRY, WE SEE HIS PERSONAL TOUCH, TIME AND AGAIN.

The world is, indeed, in a state of awful woundedness. In my Church service, I once counseled with a couple who had more than their fair share of marital challenges. On one occasion, the wife said to me, "We are just two broken people, trying our best to love each other." We are all broken; we are all wounded. Our Heavenly Parents recognize our condition and have not left us comfortless. We have a restored knowledge of the most loving, empathic, and feeling God in religious history. And we have the gift of those intimations of our soul's home in the heavens from which we came and which beckon us to return. Our work is to participate with Christ in the healing work that such faith can inspire us to enact—upon each other and upon a hurting world.

CHAPTER 4

WORLDS
WITHOUT END

In my previous life, I was a professor of literature and religion, specializing in the Romantic era. A classic poem of that period is by the poet who was reputedly David O. McKay's favorite—Robert Burns. A farmer who has just disturbed the home of a field mouse apologizes for its destruction and laments the general fragility of the natural world. But then he considers the suffering creature and decides, speaking to the mouse,

> Still, thou art blest, compar'd with me!
> The present only toucheth thee:
> But Och! I backward cast my e'e,
>   On prospects drear!
> An forward tho' I canna sea,
>   I guess an'fear![1]

We mortals may be alone among species in fearing the future. But we are also alone in possessing the gift of hope—if we are able to claim it as ours. When we find ourselves perplexed, troubled, or wounded—and most of all doubtful—it is perhaps hope that we most fervently desire. Paul speaks of love, faith, and hope as the triad of virtues most devoutly to be sought. I have focused on the doors of faith because I believe faith is the lynchpin that binds all three in a unity of durable discipleship.

Charity—pure, absolute love—is the only force in the universe stronger than self-interest. It is the indispensable motive force behind faith, the only viable catalyst, because all other motivations are a form of investment, of behavior that is merely prudent, of actions that are directly or indirectly self-seeking. Faith is manifest when we enter that realm where the present is severed from future reward or happy outcome. Another way of saying this is that faith is in someone, i.e., the Christ. It is not faith for something. It is perhaps the only occasion in which we engage the divine non-teleologically. Faith is the commitment to be responsive and true and loyal out of love in the here and now, the present moment, with no conceptualization of a tomorrow. It is the willed offering of trust in response to the call of love.

> IF FAITH IS THE TRUSTING LEAP INTO THE DARKNESS, THEN HOPE IS THE ASSURANCE YOU WILL BE CAUGHT.

Hope is not wishful thinking or simple optimism. Hope is the concrete expectation, borne of spiritual witness, of a good result. If faith is the trusting leap into the darkness, then hope is the assurance you will be caught. We generally conflate the two into the concept of faith, but faith does not know the end of the action. When Mormon returned to lead his armies, it was without any confidence in the outcome; hence, he said it was "without hope."[2] It was a gesture devoid of a conviction about the efficacy of the action.

Hope is something, according to Paul, in which we rejoice.[3] Hence, it has to be the other side of the coin of faith. Faith is the cast of the dice that only we can initiate. Hope is when we have, from outside ourselves, intimations of the outcome. Or as Paul told the Colossians, hope "grounds and settles" us after the initial gesture of faith.[4] Or again, faith is manifest in the act, it is the gesture requiring willful effort, what Paul calls the actual "work." Waiting with what he calls "patience" in anticipation of faith's fruit is the realm of "hope." This is how he explains the relationship to the Thessalonians.[5] And the engine motivating the whole sequence, he says, is charity.

I began this book with the claim that if we embrace the gospel willingly as well as wittingly, we can perceive the full beauty of God's face and will never forsake him. If we are to find the power within ourselves to respond to God's call, then we have to make the love of God more than an abstraction. Theology, to the ears of many, moves us away from the demands of practical religion into the realms of abstraction. My thesis has been the opposite. An inspired theology is the key to decode what seems random and meaningless about human history and personal experience. The Hungarian-British polymath Michael Polanyi says it differently: a "framework of beliefs enables us to hear a tune where otherwise we would hear only a noise."[6] I'd like to think that's his way of saying an inspired theological framework serves us as a door of faith, allowing us to perceive a reality of more sublime scope and beauty. As Paul said, "The world of creation cannot as yet see reality."[7]

When we invest ourselves in a story where God's love is genuinely parental with roots in premortal worlds and is the generative catalyst behind our very presence in this world, we see with new eyes. When we celebrate Eve for opening the portal to our embodiment, we can join with the Christian writer who opined, "I shall not be fool enough to suppose that trouble and pain are wholly evil parentheses in my existence but just as likely ladders to be climbed toward moral and spiritual [adult]hood."[8] When we see our failings through the eyes of Heavenly Parents who know the best as well as the most wounded parts of our soul, we can hear them say, as Julian of Norwich did, "My dear one, I am glad thou art come to me in all thy woe. I have ever been with thee and now seest thou how I love thee."[9] When we seek Christ for healing and not just our saving, self-concern is obviated. We crave wholeness so that we might be healers with him. Our eyes are then opened to see heaven not as a reward we earn or a place awarded to us but as a condition of sanctified life in sanctified relationship with others.

And yet, and yet....

What awaits you, in particular, after your passing? How well-grounded is your hope, and how might it find surer foundations? The mystic Emanuel Swedenborg may have expressed it best when he wrote that "it is [a person's] ruling love that awaits him after death. . . . Everyone has many loves; but they are all related to his ruling love."[10] How do you know what your ruling love is? It may lie so deep within that even we ourselves are—for the most part—oblivious. C. S. Lewis wrote of a time to come when "you will be forced at last to utter the speech which has lain at the center of your soul for years . . . Till that word can be dug out of us, why should [God] hear the babble that we think we mean?"[11]

My own belief is that, in large measure, our deepest, most authentic, not always conscious ruling love is the pole star toward which we incline, moment by moment. No more powerful force than love exists in the universe, and it draws us onward. That is one reason why faith must be a choice. God wants our assent freely given, not as a product of intellectual reasoning, pious self-interest, or fear and trembling. Those may be waystations along the path to him. Ultimately, and ideally, we find ourselves in a place where no certainties compel us and no impossibilities dissuade us. It seems to me obvious that everywhere we turn, we find ourselves in this vortex of competing forces that cancel each other out, leaving us free to choose. That seems to be inescapably a part of the whole design.

Francine Bennion described this Restoration understanding of moral agency at the heart of the great plan of happiness:

> God offered a profoundly different possibility, that with his help we meet and create reality as individuals in a universe of law and personal agency, and ultimately choose who we want to be, choosing to become more like himself if that is what we want, choosing to become gods if that is what we truly want for all eternity. Law in God's universe is a matter of processes or relationships that are knowable and predictable, not whimsical or inconsistent.

Such law is inherent in all matters. Agency in such a universe is not only the capacity for moral choice, but more largely, the capacity for real thought, action, and invention, with inherent consequences for oneself and others. An agent is one whose self cannot be permanently determined by other persons, or by events and circumstances.[12]

True enough, we never inhabit that ground of perfect equilibrium. Environment, upbringing, culture, and genes all have their say. But even if the dust never settles completely or the white noise never clears entirely, we find no compulsion in one direction or the other. In the inner sanctum of the soul, we have the capacity to let the compass needle of our will swing free, gently inclined to respond in that space of freedom to what Swedenborg called our ruling love. And it is then that we will choose, act, and trust or not trust the needle's gentle movement.

We are guided by our ruling love. But know this—the ruling love that guides your fate can change, does change, and is changing even now. But is it changing in the direction to give you a basis for hope? The stakes are high, as two of the most disconcerting verses in the Book of Mormon record. As we read in Jacob, "Because they desired it God hath done it."[13] And the Lord told two apostles, "ye shall both have according to your desires."[14] How do we know that when our life's review takes place, we will be found desiring and loving the right things with our affections centered in the right Being?

Anxiety is probably the most pervasive wound of our age. We worry about our families and friends. We worry about our jobs, our grades, our relationships. We worry about our future, our major, our graduation, our career choices, and our faith commitments. And having made those faith commitments, we worry about where they will take us, here and hereafter.

Historically, religious anxiety in particular has been the catalyst for some of the world's great religious revolutions. The intense human craving for relief from the fears of death and damnation gave rise to the Protestant Reformation in the person of a deeply troubled Martin Luther. Anxiety over the state of his soul led John Wesley to searching and spiritual rebirth that spawned, in turn, the Methodist church. Joseph Smith, in his 1832 First Vision account, confessed that he, too, was unsettled, anxious, and seeking some assurance of his standing before God when he entered the woods that spring morning of 1820.

When the Protestants broke with the Church of Rome, they lost the assurance that had until then been grounded in receiving the authorized church sacraments.[15] Luther found a new basis for assurance in salvation by grace alone. But we as Latter-day Saints, being neither Catholic nor evangelical, do not have either option available to us. How do we find assurance, hope, confidence, and the peace that passeth understanding as we contemplate the eternal worlds? If our ruling love awaits us, if the law of restoration guarantees that the only certainty is that our desires will find their eventual and inevitable fulfillment, how can we be sure that our love and desires will take shape as they should?

Joseph Smith restored a gospel that gives us that assurance. There is irony here because we do not generally employ terms like *omnipotent* or *omnipresent* to describe our

Heavenly Father. He is self-limiting out of respect for our agency, not a sovereign imposing his will upon the world. And he is spatially finite and embodied, not everywhere present in his own person. And yet, here is the glorious point. Our God—the weeping God of Enoch, or rather, the Heavenly Parents in whose courts our spirits resided in eons past—have the desire and the capacity to bring all of their children home to an exalted place in the eternal worlds. That was the plan from the beginning. No other prospect could have made the daughters and sons of God shout for joy.

This should be obvious. We read that "God shall wipe away all tears from their eyes; and there shall be no more death, neither sorrow, nor crying, neither shall there be any more pain."[16] But if God shall wipe away all tears, he can only do so by triumphing over the cause of those tears, which is death's severing of our most intimate family ties and connections. Any joy we savor in the absence of our loved ones is a partial joy, a fractured joy. Heaven apart from those we love is just hell by another name.

We can have confidence in the end of the story because we know how it began. We did not begin in a lost and fallen world but in a family circle, in the company of the gods. As the great mystic Julian of Norwich taught, by way of an allegory she beheld in vision, God sent Adam—and by extension all of us—"to a certain place to do his will." Not only does Adam go but he "runs off in great haste, loving to do our lord's will." Soon he falls into a ditch where he struggles in the mire, groans, and moans, but he cannot rise or help himself in any way. Julian looks to see how the Eternal Father responds to this mishap, and he tells her that only the man's good intent and great desires were "cause of

94

his falling." Therefore, he explains, "Lo, my beloved servant, what harm and distress he hath taken in service to my will! Shall I not therefore reward him for his fright and fear, his hurt and harm and all his woe?" In fact, sending him forth was "no favor" unless he be "highly and blessedly rewarded forever, *above what he would have been if he had not fallen*," culminating in "surpassing honour and endless bliss" (my emphasis).[17]

A different beginning changes the ending. The earliest Christian writers knew this. How clear and beautiful are so many of the texts from those first few Christian centuries. Origen spoke words of sweet assurance to those injured by the travails of life in what seemed at times an undeserved sea of troubles.

> All the saints who depart from this life will remain in some place situated on the earth, which holy Scripture calls paradise, as in some place of instruction, and, so to speak, class-room or school of souls. . . . If any one indeed be pure in heart, and holy in mind, . . . he will, by making more rapid progress, quickly ascend . . . and reach the kingdom of heaven. . . . And thus he will in order pass through all gradations, following Him who hath passed into the heavens, . . . who said, I will that where I am, these may be also.[18]

We might consider the most unimaginable import of those words, first spoken by Jesus Christ on the eve of his death. "Father, I want those you have given me to be with me."[19] The Son of God has expressly told us that he is desirous of our companionship in those worlds without end. Your companionship.

Exodus 33:11 records the remarkable fact that "the LORD spake unto Moses face to face, as a man speaketh unto his friend." Sadly, as the great Anglican bishop Kenneth Kirk notes, the fervent hope that the ancient Jews held, that they might actually come to see God, died out.

> Different expedients were adopted [so] that ... the implication of seeing God face to face might be evaded. . . . Throughout the sacred texts, therefore, editors developed the habit of substituting the phrase 'appear before Jahweh' or 'be seen by Jahweh' for the phrase 'see Jahweh.' . . . When therefore the Old Testament canon closed, various influences combined to dim the hope of the individual . . . that he should see [actually] God.[20]

It is clear, Kirk notes, that our Father is much more desirous of bringing us home than we have been led to believe. One rabbinic tradition tells us poignantly of God's desire to make us peers rather than subjects:

> A king went into his garden to speak to his gardener, but the gardener hid himself from him. Then said the king, "Why hidest thou from me? See I am even as thou."—So too shall God walk with the righteous in the earthly Paradise after the resurrection; and they shall see Him and quake before Him. Then shall He say unto them, "Fear not; for lo! I am even as ye."[21]

In the New Testament, something of this tender regard survives in one instance as a promise that is astounding in its depiction of a God whose love and regard surpass any expectation we might reasonably hold. In the Gospel of Luke, the Lord makes this unimaginable promise: "Blessed are those servants, whom the lord when he cometh shall find watching: verily I say unto you, that he shall gird himself, and make them to sit down to meat, and will come forth and serve them."[22]

How can we make sense of this awkward scene? The greatest religious poet of them all, George Herbert himself, struggled to accept the narrative at face value and did so only when he had imagined a conversation unfolding at that future time between a guest and his host. I believe that most of you will see yourself in the guest's words.

> Love bade me welcome. Yet my soul drew back
> > Guilty of dust and sin.
> But quick-eyed Love, observing me grow slack
> > From my first entrance in,
> Drew nearer to me, sweetly questioning,
> > If I lacked any thing.
> *A guest, I answered, worthy to be here:*
> > Love said, You shall be he.
> *I the unkind, ungrateful? Ah my dear,*
> > *I cannot look on thee.*
> Love took my hand, and smiling did reply,
> > Who made the eyes but I?
> *Truth Lord, but I have marred them: let my shame*
> > *Go where it doth deserve.*

And know you not, says Love, who bore the blame?
My dear, then I will serve.
You must sit down, says Love, and taste my
meat:
So I did sit and eat.[23]

Julian of Norwich rendered such unhoped for interaction with the divine in even greater detail, narrating a vision she had of Christ finding joy in the companionship of those he called his friends: "Then I saw the Lord . . . in His own house, . . . filling it with joy and mirth, Himself endlessly to gladden and to solace his dearworthy friends, full warmly and courteously, with marvelous melody of endless love." Then God showed her "the thanks of our Lord God" that every soul will receive "that hath willingly served God in any degree in earth." In her vision, "all the blessed creatures in heaven shall see that worshipful thanking, and he makes that soul's service known to all that are in Heaven."[24] Truly, as Joseph Smith taught, "Our heavenly Father is more liberal in His views, and boundless in His mercies and blessings, than we are ready to believe or receive."[25]

Another New Testament verse may be offering reassuring words of hope and promise, but we have missed the point because of translation choices. I refer to the famous concluding verse of the Sermon on the Mount—the injunction to be perfect. There are in this passage two moments of debatable translation choices. You probably know one of them: *teleioi*, here translated as "perfect," means more accurately, "fully realized or complete." A second point of dispute concerns the very first word, *esesthe*, which strictly speaking means "you will be." The verb is a future indicative but is—in this specific case—more often translated in biblical versions as an imperative, "Be!" A point of grammar is necessary here: Sometimes the Greek future indicative can be interpreted as a command; in which case, it is called a jussive future. However, Jesus generally uses an actual imperative when he wants to give a command as he does just four verses earlier.[26] All of this is to say, one might with equal reasonableness render Matthew 5:48 as does the Bible translator Kenneth Wuest: "Therefore, as for you, you shall be those who are complete in your character, even as your Father in heaven is complete in his being."[27] Or as another version translates the promise, "you, therefore, will be growing into spiritual maturity both in mind and character, as your heavenly Father."[28]

If these renderings are plausible, then we hear not an intimidating injunction but words of comfort, assurance, and peace. "Follow my counsels. Trust in me. Keep faith with these covenants and principles. And you will become whole and complete." So where, I ask, is the grounds for this confidence, this assurance, that "all shall be well, and all shall be well, and all manner of things shall be well"?[29] If life is a school, then we must trust the schoolmaster. I think that is the motif that pervades scripture. I think the Lord is telling us to trust that he loves us beyond imagining, that he can shape our hearts and desires in such a way that our ruling love will guide us to where he is. The key is repentance, but repentance in this scheme means the continual reeducation of the heart.

The novelist John Williams intimated as much. As he wrote of one of his characters,

In his extreme youth, [William] Stoner had thought of love as an absolute state of being to which, if one were lucky, one might find access. In his maturity he had decided it was the heaven of a false religion, toward which one ought to gaze with an amused disbelief, a gently familiar contempt, and an embarrassed nostalgia. Now in his middle age he began to know that it was neither a state of grace nor an illusion; he saw it as *a human act of becoming*, a condition that was invented and modified moment by moment and day by day, *by the will and the intelligence and the heart* [my emphases].[30]

I've not read a better characterization of love: a gradual, deliberate, willful act of fully realizing the self in relation to the other, involving intelligence as much as emotion. Along this path, we must make ourselves, in David Whyte's words, an "apprentice . . . to the difficult and fierce revelations of existence."[31] We are all apprentices, and we have good reason to trust the Master.

Agnes Callard has written an insightful study about the difference between ambition and aspiration. When we are ambitious, we seek to reap better rewards consistent with our values. When we are aspirational, we are seeking to embrace better values. Though she employs the language of philosophy, Callard captures perfectly the trust we must practice if our hearts are to be shaped in ever more beautiful directions: "Human progress in value depends on our openness to feeling some goodness before we can make reflective sense to ourselves of that goodness."[32] This call to openness, she continues, "involves opening oneself to being shaped by others: to listen, to attend, to submit oneself to the judgment of those who have a better grasp than oneself."[33]

You and I, in our particular predicament then, need confidence—or faith—of two sorts. We must trust that our divine Parents really can and really will bring each one of us home. And we need the confidence that this institution, this Church of Jesus Christ, is the optimal mechanism for assisting us in that process.

It is not fashionable in today's secular age to speak of trust in an institution. My institutional trust in the Church of Jesus Christ is rooted in my self-knowledge and in my work as a historian. Simply put, I need the Church and you, its members. I need the inspiration that comes of our shared aspirations and disappointments and struggles. I need the discipline of instruction and reminding; I need the discipline of stewardship and sacrifice and service. There are no solitary saints, and I harbor no delusions about my capacity for unassisted self-transcendence. I am not the measure of all things. I want to be taught, instructed, guided—and I believe benevolent Heavenly Parents have made provision for revealing their plan and their principles to inspired figures who have managed, however imperfectly, to pierce the veils of ignorance that blight our world. And they have revealed covenants and ordinances that tap into unseen reservoirs of spiritual light and power. Joseph knew, as I have felt, that the vicissitudes of mortality and the frailties of human commitment tend toward chaos and disintegration. Entropy appears to be a universal principle not only of thermodynamics but of civilization and human relationships. In spite of the best efforts of the most earnest individuals, marriages fail, friendships fade, and family ties falter. In priesthood and temple practices, I have experienced a power as real as the laws of physics, one that assists in the formation of more durable bonds that connect individuals to each other and to God.

And what does my study of history tell me about this institution? With each new revelation from the dust, I learn anew what Hugh Nibley wrote excitedly years ago: "The vast mass of fresh facts" and "voluminous . . . documents [that] have to do with the Primitive Church, . . . read as if they were written in defense of the Mormon claims. The weight of evidence is so overwhelming in our favor that we need only to point to it and it will plead our case with a force that no one can deny."[34] What, exactly, does early Christian history tell us? The documents reveal doctrines and practices that align, time and again, with the doctrines and practices that Joseph Smith restored. Now a skeptic might say that only demonstrates a congruence between two churches, ancient and modern. It tells us nothing about the intrinsic inspiration or truth behind either one. Perhaps. And yet, we find all around us an almost fevered rush on the part of Christian thinkers everywhere to return to these primeval principles. Let me give you more than half a dozen examples where, in case after case, what the world once called Latter-day Saint heresies have become the current orthodoxy or subject of renewed discussion.

- In interpreting the Garden story in the second century, Irenaeus found Adam and Eve's expulsion from Eden an act of mercy, not of cursing. His language eerily anticipates the precise doctrine and exact language found in Alma 42 and Latter-day Saint temple theology. He wrote,

Wherefore also He drove him out of Paradise, and removed him far from the tree of life, not because He envied him the tree of life, as some venture to assert, but because He pitied him, [and did not desire] that he should continue a sinner forever, nor that the sin which surrounded him should be immortal, and evil interminable and irremediable. But He set a bound to his [state of] sin, by interposing death, and thus causing sin to cease, putting an end to it by the dissolution of the flesh, which should take place in the earth, so that man, ceasing at length to live to sin, and dying to it, might begin to live to God.[35]

- *Teachings of the Twelve Apostles* (*The Didache*), a late first- or early second-century manual for Christian communities, clearly described baptism as an adult ordinance, children implicitly having no need, being free from sin.[36] Latter-day Saints denied the original guilt and damnation of unbaptized children in 1830. It would take almost two more centuries before Pope Benedict's 2007 document "The Hope of Salvation for Infants Who Die Without Being Baptized." In that text, Catholic authorities express the hope—but not the assurance—that unbaptized infants are not damned.[37]

- In the second century, Clement taught that "the Word of God became man, that thou mayest learn from man how man may become God."[38] He turns possible figure of speech to actual destiny when he writes that "those who have become perfect . . . are called by the appellation of gods, being destined to sit on thrones with the other gods that have been first put in their places by the Saviour."[39] Basil the Great (330–79) also celebrated the prospect not just of "being made like to God" but "highest of all, the being made God," as did Gregory Nazianzen (ca. 329– ca. 390).[40] Latter-day Saints preached a robust version of theosis and were vehemently attacked in 1838 for their blasphemy. Now, one finds a mainstream journal like *Christianity Today* urging how "The Strange Yet Familiar Doctrine of Theosis Can Reinvigorate the Christian Life."[41]

- Origen, in the third century, taught that "the education of the soul is an age-long spiritual adventure, beginning in this life and continuing after death."[42] And so Joseph Smith reveals a progressive, tiered salvation, but he did so several generations before Karl Barth asked, "If God's . . . saving will is supreme, how is eternal loss possible?"[43]

- Also in the third century, pseudo-Clement put the question to Peter, "Shall then those be wholly deprived of the kingdom who have died before His coming?"[44] The Latter-day Saints recovered a scheme of salvation for all the living and the dead a century or more before Pope John Paul II spoke of universal salvation and before Rob Bell asked about the uncatechized, "What if the missionary gets a flat tire?"[45]

- Origen also taught that "the Father himself is not without suffering. When he is prayed to, he has pity and compassion; he suffers something of love . . . and on account of us he endures human sufferings."[46] Yet the weeping God that Joseph Smith revealed in 1830 was starkly blasphemous in the face of every Christian creed extant in Smith's lifetime. Then, beginning at the end of the nineteenth century, there began a stampede to embrace that very conception, a God the Father who feels and experiences passions.

• In a related development, more than one theologian is now arguing that "if God is passible, . . . he should be corporeal as well. Christian theology does not exclude in advance all possible forms of divine embodiment, and . . . it seems possible to develop a theory of divine corporeality . . . compatible with the basic tenets of Christian theology."[47] Scholars now acknowledge the startling fact that "divine embodiment would have been part of the theological mainstream prior to Origen and Augustine."[48] A recent book, *God's Body*, goes so far as to say that, at the present moment, a critique of the Platonic hostility to divine embodiment that dominated Christianity in the subsequent centuries is "in vogue."[49]

• Finally, Joseph's restoration of temple worship and temple theology was roundly condemned as bizarre and un-Christian. What a difference a few dozen decades make. Now Marcus von Wellnitz notes the obvious fact that "the early Christians" engaged in the dual worship of meeting house and temple,[50] and as S. G. F. Brandon writes, "There is an abundance of evidence that [early] Christians continued faithful in their reverence for the temple and in their observance of its [worship forms]."[51]

It is becoming ever clearer that the Latter-day Saints didn't deviate from early Christianity; Christianity deviated from early Christianity, and now it is in many regards returning. A growing chorus of scholars recognize that many of the foundations of modern Christianity, those laid by Augustine especially, were not extenuations of orthodoxy but deviations from orthodoxy. In Henry Chadwick's words, the Pelagius who was condemned as a heretic was "a traditionalist, defending the true faith against the innovations of Augustine."[52] B. R. Rees notes that when monks not only in faraway Marseilles but even in Roman Africa read Augustine on original sin and his attacks on free will, "they were deeply shocked."[53] He was not expounding orthodoxy: he was creating it. Elizabeth Clark writes that the twin condemnation of Pelagius and Origen ensured the supremacy "of a Christian theology whose central concerns were human sinfulness, not human potentiality; divine determination, not human freedom and responsibility; God's mystery, not God's justice. *Christianity was perhaps poorer for their suppression*" (my emphasis).[54]

Maybe those shifting judgments are of purely historical interest. I find them compelling evidence of divine inspiration working through a remarkable, prophetic, nineteenth-century mind to recuperate and expand upon an original Christian gospel.

But these examples are not where my principal hope finds its primary ground.

Even from the valleys of uncertainty, I am profoundly and deeply moved by the specter of a young, itinerant Galilean rabbi who, two thousand years ago, willingly offered himself up to barbaric execution, enduring unspeakable torment because he believed that—by so doing—he was offering me, personally, respite from the pains and humiliations and failures and wounds of my life whether inflicted by others or by my own deliberate, foolish choices. As the Book of Mormon testified would happen, I find myself "drawn" to this unparalleled act of grace and unfathomable kindness to me.[55] Before his divinity or Lordship, his virgin birth or his resurrection, I am confronted with the brute, historic fact of that Galilean rabbi dying on a cross because he believed his death would enhance my life. Though he is my Redeemer and my Healer and my God, I find the response that precedes any act of faith is my response to an act of selfless, unmerited love by a flesh and blood individual who lived twenty centuries ago.

That is where I first confront the truth about love. It is a truth most eloquently articulated by Kenneth Kirk: "Three things are true about love," he wrote.

> The first is, that it always confers independence upon the object of its love. It gives, compelling no return; it goes on giving, though no love is given in answer. It is the one force in the world which does not bargain. . . . Second, if love endows the *recipient* with formal freedom—with the right to accept or reject at will—it also, and it alone, confers upon the *giver* actual freedom. . . . In love and in love alone can [humankind] actualize the freedom . . . which God has given him. . . . Man becomes free as he learns to love. And finally, love is irresistible. . . . And therefore whatever in the end opposes it must in the end give way. . . . The same power which confers freedom on its recipients also evokes from them—not

by contract, not by force, but by the invincible suasion of a moral appeal—an answer of love freely given in return.[56]

I therefore take as scripture the words of Clement, who believed—as I do—that "we can set no limits to the agency of the Redeemer; to redeem, to rescue, to discipline, is his work, and so will he continue to operate after this life."[57] That sentiment was echoed by a modern prophet, Joseph F. Smith, who said,

> Jesus had not finished his work when his body was slain, neither did he finish it after his resurrection from the dead; although he had accomplished the purpose for which he then came to the earth, he had not fulfilled all his work. And when will he? Not until he has redeemed and saved every son and daughter of our father Adam that have been or ever will be born upon this earth to the end of time, except the sons of perdition. That is his mission.[58]

Jesus Christ is committed to shaping our hearts and shaping our love to align with his. I trust in his patience and his power to do so. That is the source of my confidence and my hope. I worship a Christ who wants peers, not subjects. Friends, not servants. He comes as our healer, not our judge. If you don't believe that, listen to John the Beloved. He wrote, "For God did not send His Son to the world in order to judge the world, but in order to heal the world."[59] My heart resonates to the truth of Thomas Traherne's words: "He delighteth in our happiness more than we; and is of all others the most lovely object. An infinite Lord, who having all riches, honors, and pleasures in his own hand, is infinitely willing to give them unto me. Which is the fairest idea that can be devised."[60]

Insofar as there is judgment, according to the apostle Paul, it will be a process of helpful assessment to prepare us for progress to the next stage of our growth. As he taught the Corinthians, "Being judged, we are corrected by the Lord, *that we not be* condemned" (my emphasis).[61] This is what Elder Dieter Uchtdorf seems to have meant when he said, "That Day of Judgment will be a day of mercy and love—a day when broken hearts are healed, when tears of grief are replaced with tears of gratitude, when all will be made right."[62] As for hell, I trust the words of James Talmage, who wrote that "no man will be kept in hell [spirit prison] longer than is necessary to bring him to a fitness for something better. When he reaches that stage the prison doors will open and there will be rejoicing among the hosts who welcome him into a better state."[63]

My profession of belief and of hope is that only a God who can redeem all of his creation is worthy of adoration, and that is the God rediscovered by Joseph Smith. I believe the words of Christ when he told his disciples upon leaving them that he would be at work preparing our abode in the worlds without end and that he desires us to be with him there. And I have hope we will find ourselves there because Christ's love for each one of us, whom he knows by name, will ultimately prove irresistible.

In my own personal odyssey, I have grown ever more confident of the essential goodness and beauty of an underlying purpose and trajectory behind our lives. My study of theology persuades me that Joseph Smith provided a cosmic narrative of incomparable moral and logical coherence. I have felt a degree of love and light that transcends anything human and conclude it has its source in the Eternal. Surpassing as it does any human categories, only imagination can provide a semblance of its fulness. Anything we can conceive that is unfailingly benevolent and good therefore, if not ultimate truth, is certainly a movement toward that Truth. Even the most beautiful scenario we can imaginatively construct, in other words, cannot possibly be too generous or hopeful, a pale simulacrum of a destiny devised by Heavenly Parents of infinite love and power.

I conclude with two final thoughts. Hope is not complacency. We have to bring Christ's work of at-one-ment to fruition by living lives of commitment and exertion and teachability. Only with our trusting cooperation can he shape the love that rules our lives, what Gerard Manley Hopkins called our "soul's star."[64] But trust that that work is even now underway.

And second, I pray you will develop a voracious appetite for the feast already laid before you. Be open to an abundant life which beckons through the doors of faith. Even philosopher Arthur Schopenhauer—no Christian idealist he!—recognized the perils of confusing our cramped perspective on reality with the whole panorama: "Every [person] takes the limits of [their] own field of vision for the limits of the world."[65] Don't let that be your error. Be open and teachable and receptive to the bounties, spiritual and material, of the here and now. The Savior said, "I am come that they might have life, and that they might have it more abundantly."[66] The key Greek word here is "*perisone*," which means "full

to overflowing," "present in superabundance." Our God is a
God of superabundance as described by the poet Robinson
Jeffers:

> Is it not by his high superfluousness we know
> Our God? For to be equal a need
> Is natural, . . . but to fling
> Rainbows over the rain
> And beauty above the moon, and secret rainbows
> On the domes of deep sea-shells,
> And make the necessary embrace of breeding
> Beautiful also as fire,
> Not even the weeds to multiply without
>   blossom
> Nor the birds without music.[67]

May you take Charles Darwin as your model in this one
regard: Be as passionately receptive to beauty and variety
and wonder as he was. When he was a student, he was already in love with the adventure of learning. His greatest
passion was collecting beetles. He recorded in his journal,

> I will give a proof of my zeal: one day, on tearing
> off some old bark, I saw two rare beetles and seized
> one in each hand; then I saw a third and new kind,
> which I could not bear to lose, so that I popped the
> one which I held in my right hand into my mouth.
> Alas it ejected some intensely acrid fluid, which
> burnt my tongue so that I was forced to spit the
> beetle out, which was lost, as well as the third one.[68]

Do whatever is required to make room for the third beetle. Enlarge your heart and mind. Enlarge your trust, your faith, your hope. Make room for that third beetle.

Epilogue

When Joseph revealed his greatest revelation, referred to for many decades as simply "The Vision" (section 76 of the Doctrine and Covenants), many members defected from the Church. The scope of God's plan was too ambitious, too generous, too magnanimous for a people raised in a Christian tradition that had long inculcated concepts of a universal Fall, limited atonement, and a severely restricted heaven. "There is a thing," wrote G. K. Chesterton, "as a small and cramped eternity. You may see it in many modern religions."[1] Joseph Smith's embrace of the premortality of the human soul, his vision of an exaltation and theosis open to all, his confidence in a future of eternal growth and progression—all are susceptible to the charge, if not of blasphemy, of a dangerous collapse of sacred distance, a risky diminution of reverence before God's transcendent holiness. But for early Saints like Parley P. Pratt, the invitation to fellowship with the gods was cause for unalloyed celebration of God's superabundance, his unstinting thirst for peers rather than subjects.

What a glorious field of intelligence now lies before us, yet but partially explored. What a boundless expanse for contemplation and reflection now opens to our astonished vision. What an intellectual banquet spreads itself invitingly to our appetite, calling into lively exercise every power and faculty of the mind, and giving full scope to all the great and ennobling passions of the soul. . . . All the virtuous principles of the human mind may here expand and grow, and flourish, unchecked by any painful emotions or gloomy fears.[2]

One complaint finds expression in the sermons of Joseph Smith, time and time again. He was perpetually frustrated by the overly modest dimensions of the human imagination, our inability—or unwillingness—to embrace the dazzling possibilities to which the gospel points us. In his language, our greatest error in conceiving of the divine was what he called "set[ting] up stakes and set[ting] bounds to the works and ways of the almighty."[3] Don't make that mistake. The prophet Joseph Smith reminds me of the great Jewish philosopher Spinoza. One of his recent biographers wrote, "He rejected the orthodoxy of his day not because he believed less, but because he believed more."[4] That, in a nutshell, is my challenge to you. Be as voracious as Mercy's father in the monumental work of Virginia Sorensen, *A Little Lower than the Angels*. Incredulous at her father's capacity for belief, Mercy had asked enviously as a child, "'But you believe it, Father, you really do?' 'I believe all I can, Mercy girl, all I can. Everywhere I go I'm looking for more good things to believe. Even if it's the be-all and the end-all here, then we'd better keep busy believing good things. Hadn't we?'"[5] That's the kind of voracious appetite I am talking about.

The great religious scholar Krister Stendahl once said we should judge any religion by its best, not its worst. At its worst, our culture can be anti-intellectual, judgmental, authoritarian, and shallow. But I love it for what is best in it: the total commitment it invites, its optimistic assessment of human potential, and the most generous God in the religious universe, one who is willing to shepherd every human soul without exception to his own exalted status as a holy being living in holy relationships. I am grateful for the Restoration's shattering of the snow globe of self-concern and of a world narrowly demarcated by birth and death. I know there are "more things in heaven and earth . . . than are dreamt of in [our] philosophy."[6] Stepping through the doors of faith has opened my eyes and my heart to profoundly satisfying answers to the most urgent questions of my existence and to an ambitious project of Zion-building here and hereafter that I judge worthy of a life of devotion. Ultimately, I gladly embrace the risk. With George MacDonald, I am willing to "fall off the same precipice with Jesus and John and Paul and a thousand more, who were lovely in their lives, and with their death make even the nothingness into which they have passed like the garden of the Lord. I will go farther, and say I would rather die forevermore believing as Jesus believed, than live forevermore as those that deny him."[7]

Notes

FOREWORD

1. Cited in "Aims of a BYU Education," Brigham Young University, up-dated 2019, https://aims.byu.edu/aims-of-a-byu-education.

2. William Johnson Cory, *Eton Reform* (London: Longman, Green, Longman, & Roberts, 1861), 6–7. Quoted in Henry Rosovsky, *The University: An Owner's Manual* (New York: W. W. Norton, 1991), 108.

3. William Wordsworth, "Ode on Intimations of Immortality from Recollections of Early Childhood," line 9.

INTRODUCTION

1. This book is an expanded version of four public lectures delivered at Brigham Young University in 2019. I thank Faith Matters for per-mission to include some material that appeared in Fiona and Terryl Givens, *All Things New: Rethinking Sin, Salvation, and Everything in Between* (Meridian, ID: Faith Matters, 2020).

2. Reinhold Niebuhr, *The Nature and Destiny of Man: A Christian Interpretation* (Ann Arbor: University of Michigan Press, 1955), 272.

3. Clement of Rome, *First Epistle of Clement to the Corinthians* (Savage, MN: Lighthouse, 2019), 29.

4. Moses 6:54.

5. Abr. 3:25.

6. Noah Webster, *An American Dictionary of the English Language* (New York: S. Converse, 1828), s.v. "prove."

NOTES

7. Nassim Nicholas Taleb, *Antifragile: Things That Gain from Disorder* (New York: Random House, 2012), 3–4.

8. Taleb, *Antifragile*, 8.

9. David Eagleman, *Livewired: The Inside Story of the Ever-Changing Brain* (New York: Vintage, 2021), 3.

10. Eagleman, *Livewired*, 4.

11. "The Church exists for nothing else but to draw men into Christ, to make them little Christs. If they are not doing that, all the cathedrals, clergy, missions, sermons, even the Bible itself, are simply a waste of time. God became Man for no other purpose. It is even doubtful, you know, whether the whole universe was created for any other purpose." C. S. Lewis, *Mere Christianity* (New York: Simon & Schuster Touchstone, 1996), 171.

12. William Wordsworth, "Lines Written a Few Miles Above Tintern Abbey; On Revisiting the Banks of the Wye During a Tour, July 13, 1798," in *Lyrical Ballads* (Bristol: Biggs and Cottle, 1798), 203.

13. "The prayer preceding all prayers is, 'May it be the real I who speaks. May it be the real Thou that I speak to.'" C. S. Lewis, *Letters to Malcolm: Chiefly on Prayer* (New York: Harcourt, 1964), 82.

14. Eagleman, *Livewired*, 10, 234, 20.

CHAPTER 1

1. Elisa V. Hunter, "What Positive Psychologists and Mormons Can Learn from Each Other," in *Master of Applied Positive Psychology Capstone Projects* (Philadelphia: University of Pennsylvania, 2013).

2. John 6:66.

3. Thomas Traherne, *Centuries of Meditations*, in *The Works of Thomas Traherne*, ed. Jan Ross (Cambridge: D. S. Drewer, 2013), 90.

4. Gregory Nazianzus, "On the Words of the Gospel," oration 37, in Philip Schaff and Henry Wace, eds., *Nicene and Post-Nicene Fathers*, 2nd ser. [*NPNF2*] (Peabody, MA: Hendrickson, 1994), 7:338–39.

5. John Milton, "Aeropagitica," in *The Prose Works of John Milton* (London: W. Ball, 1838), 113.

6. John Stuart Mill, "On Liberty," in *The Basic Writings of John Stuart Mill* (New York: Random House, 2002), 36–37.

7. Gen. 4:1.

8. 1 Ne. 11:16.

9. Alma 5:14, 26.

10. Irenaeus, *Against Heresies* V.I.1, in Alexander Roberts and James

Donaldson, eds., *The Ante-Nicene Fathers* [*ANF*] (Grand Rapids, MI: Eerdmans, 1977) 1:527.

11. Emanuel Swedenborg, *Heaven and Its Wonders and Hell: From Things Heard and Seen*, trans. John Ager (n.p.: Aziloth Books, 2011), 231–32.

12. The philosopher Blaise Pascal argued that because the post-mortal payout is eternal pain or joy and the investment only a temporal dedication to the good, it made mathematical sense to bet on the reality of God and judgment.

13. Prov. 16:3.

14. Moroni 7:48.

15. Quoted in Donald Staheli, "Obedience—Life's Great Challenge," *Ensign* 28, no. 5 (May 1998): 82.

16. Mosiah 5:13.

17. Alma 37:36.

18. John Smith, "The True Way or Method of Attaining Divine Knowledge," in *Select Discourses by John Smith*, ed. Henry Griffin Williams, 4th ed. (Cambridge: Cambridge University Press, 1859), 3.

19. John 17:3.

20. Rev. 21:5.

21. Acts 14:27.

22. 2 Ne. 26:33.

23. C. S. Lewis, *Perelandra* (New York: Scribner Classics, 1996), 16–17.

24. JS—H 1:20; Alma 5:7; Acts 9:18.

25. William Wordsworth, "The Excursion," bk. 4, l. 1157 in *The Collected Poems of William Wordsworth* (London: Wordsworth Editions, 2006), 971.

26. Moses 7:41.

27. Eugene England, "Enduring," in *Dialogues with Myself* (Midvale, UT: Orion Books, 1984), 204.

28. Cited in Ziya Tong, *The Reality Bubble: Blind Spots, Hidden Truths, and the Dangerous Illusions that Shape Our World* (New York: Penguin Random House, 2019), frontispiece.

29. Tong, *Reality Bubble*, 74.

30. Tong, *Reality Bubble*, 79–80. Tong notes that some of these individuals were actually recruited as coast watchers in WWII since they could detect signaling from UV lamps of enemy ships.

31. Cited in Tong, *Reality Bubble*, 344.

32. Tong, *Reality Bubble*, 339.

33. Quoted in Marcelo Gleiser, *Island of Knowledge* (New York: Basic Books, 2014), xiii.

34. Gleiser, *Island*, xiii–xiv.

35. William A. Luijpen, *Phenomenology and Humanism* (Pittsburgh: Duquesne University Press, 1966), 65.

36. David Hume, *A Treatise of Human Nature* (London: Penguin, 1969), 462.

37. Frances Young, *God's Presence: A Contemporary Recapitulation of Early Christianity* (Cambridge: Cambridge University Press, 2013), 38–39.

38. Jordan Peterson, *Beyond Order: 12 More Rules for Life* (New York: Penguin, 2021), xxvii.

39. Ralph Waldo Emerson, "Nature," in *Essays*, 2nd ser. (Cambridge, MA: Houghton Mifflin, 1883), 182.

40. David Deutsch, *The Beginning of Infinity: Explanations That Transform the World* (New York: Viking, 2011), 353–56.

41. Thomas Nagel, *Mind and Cosmos* (New York: Oxford University Press, 2012), 53.

42. Cited in Elliott Sober, "The Evolution of Rationality," *Synthese* 46, no. 1 (January 1981): 95.

43. Richard Feldman, "Rationality, Reliability, and Natural Selection," *Philosophy of Science* 55, no. 2 (June 1988): 218.

44. Dietrich von Hildebrand, *The Heart: An Analysis of Human and Divine Affectivity* (South Bend, IN: St. Augustine's Press, 2007), 135.

45. Frans de Waal, *Mama's Last Hug: Animal Emotions and What They Tell Us about Ourselves* (New York: Norton, 2019), 205.

46. Alma 32:35.

47. Gen. 3:6.

48. C. S. Lewis, "Learning in War-Time," in *The Weight of Glory* (New York: HarperOne, 2009), 49.

49. 2 Ne. 2:22.

50. 2 Ne. 2:11.

51. D&C 46:13.

52. D&C 93:1.

53. 3 Ne. 12:2; John 20:29.

54. 2 Ne. 2:16.

55. I made these points previously in Terryl Givens, "'Lightning Out

NOTES

of Heaven': Joseph Smith and the Forging of Community," forum address, Brigham Young University, November 29, 2005, https://speeches.byu.edu/talks/terryl-l-givens/joseph-smith-forging-community/.

56. John Keats, *Complete Poetical Works*, ed. Horace Elisha Scudder (Boston: Houghton Mifflin, 1899), 363.

57. Elaine Pagels, *Adam, Eve, and the Serpent* (New York: Vintage, 1989), 99. She attributes the principle's demise to Augustine.

CHAPTER 2

1. Ne. 13:32, 1830 edition. The 1837 and present editions replace "state of awful woundedness" with "awful state of blindness." The common point of both descriptive words is telling: woundedness and blindness alike describe a condition for which we are not responsible; the injury is due to the agency of others who have removed "plain and precious" things from the scriptural record.

2. Jan Shipps, *Mormonism: The Story of a New Religious Tradition* (Urbana: University of Illinois Press, 1987).

3. The theme of a weeping or vulnerable God, and other innovations discussed here and in subsequent pages, borrow in part from Terryl and Fiona Givens, *The God Who Weeps: How Mormonism Makes Sense of Life* (Salt Lake City, UT: Deseret Book, 2012) and Terryl and Fiona Givens, *The Christ Who Heals: How God Restored the Truth that Saves Us* (Salt Lake City, UT: Deseret Book, 2017).

4. JS—H 1:19. This 1838 account, unlike Smith's earlier 1832 narrative, emphasized the significance of the Restoration in dispensational history rather than the personal remission of his sins foregrounded in 1832.

5. "That which is without body or parts is nothing." Andrew F. Ehat and Lyndon W. Cook, eds., *The Words of Joseph Smith* (Orem, UT: Grandin Book Company, 1991), 60. Warren Cowdery criticized the Methodists for believing in a deity "without body or parts" in an 1836 Church article. *Messenger and Advocate* 2, no. 5 (February 1836): 265. Mormons, Pratt affirmed without apology, "worship a God, who has both body and parts; who has eyes, mouth, and ears, and who speaks when He pleases." Parley P. Pratt, *Mormonism Unveiled: Zion's Watchman Unmasked* (New York: Pratt and Fordham, 1838), 31.

6. Jaroslav Pelikan and Valerie Hotchkiss, eds., *Creeds and Confessions of Faith in the Christian Tradition* (New Haven, CT: Yale University Press, 2003), 2:608.

7. F. L. Cross and E. A. Livingstone, eds., "Impassibility of God," in *Oxford Dictionary of the Christian Church* (New York: Oxford University Press, 1997), 823. In contradistinction to the creedal orthodoxy of the past, the same source notes, "In the 20th century Divine impassibility has been challenged by philosophers as incoherent."

8. Augustine, *De Diversis Quaestionibus ad Simplicianum*, in Nicolas Wolterstorff, "Suffering Love," ed. William E. Mann, *Augustine's Confessions: Critical Essays* (Lanham, MD: Rowman and Littlefield, 2006), 122.

9. Thomas Aquinas, "The Summa Theologica," in *Basic Writings of St. Thomas Aquinas*, ed. Anton C. Pegis (Indianapolis: Hackett Publishing, 1997), 1:226.

10. Noah Webster, *An American Dictionary of the English Language* (New York: S. Converse, 1828), s.v. "passion." In theological terms, a passionless God means God is not perturbed or moved by outside events. The distinction from a God who does not feel our pain seems largely pedantic.

11. The words are from Anselm (1033–1109), chap. 8 in *Proslogion*, quoted in Mann, *Confessions*, 120; spelling modernized.

12. Tertullian, *The Writings*, ed. Anthony Uyl (Ontario, Canada: Devoted Publishing, 2017), 1:36.

13. Thomas Watson, "Man's Chief End is to Glorify God," in *A Body of Practical Divinity* (Philadelphia: T. Wardle, 1833), 8.

14. Roger E. Olson, *The Story of Christian Theology* (Downers Grove, IL: InterVarsity Press, 1999), 506.

15. *The Catechism of Christian Doctrine: Prepared and Enjoined by Order of the Third Plenary Council of Baltimore* (Philadelphia: Cunningham and Son, 1885) became the standard catechism in American Catholic schools.

16. Rick Warren, *The Purpose Driven Life: What on Earth Am I Here For?* (Grand Rapids, MI: Zondervan, 2012), 53.

17. John Piper, *The Pleasures of God* (Colorado Springs: Multnomah Books, 2012), 29, 192.

18. Dwight Sereno Edwards, ed., *The Works of President Edwards: With a Memoir of His Life. . .* (New York: Carvill, 1830), 1:172–73.

19. Edward Beecher, *The Concord of Ages* (New York: Derby & Jackson, 1860), 156.

20. "Lectures on Faith," D&C, 1835 ed., 39.

21. Job 7:17.

22. Sigmund Freud, *Civilization and Its Discontents*, trans. and ed. James Strachey (New York: W.W. Norton & Company, 2010), 30.

23. Moses 7:28–37.

24. 2 Ne. 2:25.

25. Ehat and Cook, *Words of Joseph Smith*, 247.

26. Theodore M. Burton, "A Marriage to Last through Eternity," *Ensign*, June 1987, https://www.churchofjesuschrist.org/study/ensign/1987/06/a-marriage-to-last-through-eternity?lang=eng.

27. Thomas Weinandy, "Does God Suffer?," *First Things*, November 2001, https://www.firstthings.com/article/2001/11/does-god-suffer.

28. Nicholas Wolterstorff, *Lament for a Son* (Grand Rapids, MI: Eerdmans, 1987), 81.

29. Ronald Goetz, "The Suffering God: The Rise of a New Orthodoxy," *Christian Century* (1986): 385.

30. Paul L. Gavrilyuk, *The Suffering of the Impassible God: The Dialectics of Patristic Thought* (New York: Oxford University Press, 2004), 1.

31. Moses 6:51.

32. For a comprehensive treatment of this topic, see Terryl Givens, *When Souls Had Wings: Premortal Life in Western Thought* (New York: Oxford University Press, 2010).

33. Plato's *Meno* contains his most famous argument, in which he leads a slave boy to recapitulate the Pythagorean theorem without having learned it in this life.

34. Plato, *Phaedrus* 250d–251b, trans. Alexander Nehamas and Paul Woodruff, in *Plato: Complete Works*, ed. John M. Cooper (Indianapolis: Hackett, 1997), 528.

35. Plato, *Symposium* 192c–d, trans. Alexander Nehamas and Paul Woodruff, in *Plato*, 475.

36. Augustine, *Confessions* X.18, trans. F. H. Sheed (Indianapolis: Hackett, 2006), 204.

37. Christina Baldwin, *The Seven Whispers* (Navato, CA: New World Library, 2002), 40–41.

38. Origen, *Against Celsus* viii.xii (n.p.: Ex Fontibus, 2016), 599.

39. Origen, *On First Principles* III.vi.6, trans. G. W. Butterworth (New York: Harper & Row, 1966), 251.

40. See Terryl Givens, *Wrestling the Angel: The Foundations of Mormon Thought: Cosmos, God, Humanity* (New York: Oxford University Press, 2015), 58.

41. Origen, *Homilies 1–14 on Ezekiel 6.6*, ed. D. D. McManus, trans. Thomas P. Scheck (New York: Newman Press, 2010), 92–93.

42. Origen, *Homilies on Numbers 27.11*, in Antonia Tripolitis, *Doctrine of the Soul in the Thought of Plotinus and Origen* (Roslyn Heights, NY: Libra, 1977), 126; and *De Principiis* II.xi.6–7 paraphrased in Tripolitis, *Doctrine of the Soul*, 133.

43. Henri Crouzel, *Origen*, trans. A. S. Worrall (San Francisco: Harper & Row, 1989), xi.

44. Philip Schaff, *History of the Christian Church*, 8 vols. (Grand Rapids, MI: Eerdmans, 1910), 3:699.

45. Joseph Wilson Trigg, *Origen: The Bible and Philosophy in the Third-century Church* (Atlanta: John Knox Press, 1983), 8.

46. Henry More, "The Preexistence of the Soul," in *The Complete Poems of Dr. Henry More* (Lancashire, England: for private circulation, 1878), 128.

47. Henry More, *Philosophical Writings of Henry More*, ed. Flora Isabel MacKinnon (New York: Oxford University Press, 1925), 9.

48. Henry More, "Pre-Existence," in *Light* (London: Eclectic Publishing, 1887), 7:587.

49. Benjamin Whichcote, "The First Sermon," in *Select Sermons of Dr. Whichcot* (London: Awnsham and John Churchill, 1698), 5.

50. Nathanael Culverwel, *An Elegant and Learned Discourse on the Light of Nature* (1652), in E. T. Campagnac, *The Cambridge Platonists* (Oxford: Clarendon Press, 1901), 255.

51. Culverwel, *Discourse*, in Campagnac, *Cambridge Platonists*, 290.

52. Immanuel Kant, *Critique of Practical Reason*, trans. Thomas Kingsmill Abbott (New York: Cosimo Classics, 2008), 170.

53. Immanuel Kant, *Critique of Pure Reason* (London: Henry G. Bohn, 1885), 474.

54. Julius Müller, *The Christian Doctrine of Sin*, 2 vols., trans. William Urwick (Edinburgh: Clark, 1868), 2:234–35.

55. See the discussion and references in Givens, *When Souls Had Wings*, 282–84.

56. Marilynne Robinson, *Absence of Mind: The Dispelling of Inwardness from the Modern Myth of the Self* (New Haven, CT: Yale University Press, 2010), 110.

57. George MacDonald, *A Book of Strife in the Form of the Diary of an Old Soul* (London: Arthur C. Fifield, 1905).

58. Marcel Proust, *Remembrance of Things Past*, trans. G. K. Scott Moncrieff (New York: Random House, 1927), 2:509–10.

59. *Homo Viator: Introduction to a Metaphysic of Hope*, trans. Emma Craufurd (Chicago: Henry Regnery, 1951), 8.

60. Clement of Alexandria, *Instructor* I.6, in Alexander Roberts and James Donaldson, eds., *The Ante-Nicene Fathers [ANF]* (Grand Rapids, MI: Eerdmans, 1977), 2:217.

61. In Elizabeth Shepley Sergeant, *Robert Frost: The Trial by Existence* (New York: Holt, Rhinehart and Winston, 1960).

62. Dorothy Sayers, *The Mind of the Maker: The Expression of Faith through Creativity and Art* (London: Methuen, 1941), 110–11.

63. Brigham Young in Brigham Young et al., *Journal of Discourses [JD]*, 26 vols., reported by G. D. Watt et al. (Liverpool: F. D. and S. W. Richards, et al., 1851–86; repr., Salt Lake City, UT: n.p., 1974), 7:1–8.

CHAPTER 3

1. John 20:25–28.

2. 1 Ne. 21:16.

3. Cardinal Walter Kasper, *Mercy: The Essence of the Gospel and the Key to Christian Life* (Mahwah, NJ: Paulist Press, 2014), 44.

4. William Harmless, ed., *Augustine in His Own Words* (Washington, DC: Catholic University Press, 2010), 387.

5. Lord Byron, *Cain*, 1.1.lxv-lviii.

6. Irenaeus, *Against Heresies* IV.xxxix.1, in *ANF* 1:522.

7. S. M. K. [Sarah M. Kimball], "Plea for the Women of Massachusetts and Mother Eve, vs. Kate Bowers," *Woman's Exponent* 2, no. 18 (February 15, 1874): 141. Cited in Boyd J. Petersen, "'Redeemed from the Curse Placed Upon Her': Dialogic Discourse on Eve in the *Women's Exponent*," *Journal of Mormon History* 40, no. 1 (Winter 2014): 155–56.

8. Ehat and Cook, *Words of Joseph Smith*, 360.

9. Young, *JD*, 3:47.

10. David Epstein, *Range: Why Generalists Triumph in a Specialized World* (New York: Riverhead, 2019), 35.

11. Epstein, *Range*, 21.

12. Epstein, *Range*, 30.

13. Epstein, *Range*, 34.

14. 1 Ne. 12:22.

15. A. D. Lindsay, *The Two Moralities: Our Duty to God and to Society* (London: Eyre & Spottiswoode, nd), 49. Cited in Sayers, *Mind of the Maker*, 155.

16. John Harris, "Risk and Terror," *Dialogue: A Journal of Mormon Thought* 26, no. 4 (Winter 1993): 155.

17. Young, *JD*, 3:316; 19:41.

18. Thomas O'Dea, *The Mormons* (Chicago: University of Chicago, 1957), 151–52. O'Dea attributes the phrase "vigorous exercise of the will" to an unnamed "Mormon thinker."

19. James 1:5; JS—H 1:13, 26.

20. He is "merciful, and gracious, slow to anger, long suffering, and full of goodness. . . . Those who know their weakness and liability to sin, would be in constant doubt of salvation, if it were not for the idea which they have of the . . . character of God. . . . An idea of these facts does away doubt, and makes faith exceeding strong." "Lectures on Faith," D&C, 1835 ed., 39.

21. In Richard John Neuhaus, *Catholic Matters: Confusion, Controversy, and the Splendor of Truth* (New York: Basic Books, 2006), 13.

22. Austen Farrer, *Essential Sermons* (Cambridge, MA: Cowley Publications, 1991), 86.

23. David Bentley Hart, *The New Testament* (New Haven, CT: Yale University Press, 2017), introduction.

24. Acts 15:1, 10.

25. Young, *JD*, 8:185.

26. Mark 6:31.

27. Mark 7:33.

28. Mark 8:22–23.

29. Mark 9:2.

30. 1 Ne. 11:17.

31. William Shakespeare, *Hamlet*, 1.5.167–68.

32. Moses 1:10.

33. D&C 137:6.

34. 2 Kings 6:17.

35. 2 Cor. 12:2.

36. D&C 49:8.

37. Isa. 33:14.

38. Richard Feynman, cited in John W. Casperson, *A Chalice of Miracles* (Bloomington, IN: AuthorHouse, 2008), 532.

39. John Gribbin, *Schrödinger's Kittens and the Search for Reality* (New York: Back Bay Books, 1996), 16.

40. John Gribbin, *In Search of Schrödinger's Cat: Quantum Physics and Reality* (New York: Bantam Books, 1984), 92.

41. Gary Zukav, *The Dancing Wu Li Masters: An Overview of the New Physics* (New York: HarperOne, 2009), 220.

42. Ethan Siegel, "Quantum Physics Is Fine, Human Bias About Reality Is The Real Problem," *Forbes* (September 11, 2019), https://www.forbes.com/sites/startswithabang/2019/09/11/the-most-unpopular-interpretation-of-quantum-physics-may-make-all-the-others-irrelevant/?sh=566c3cfb6444.

43. Gribbin, *In Search of Schödinger's Cat*, 236–37.

44. George Musser, *Spooky Action at a Distance: The Phenomenon that Reimagines Space and Time—and What It Means for Black Holes, the Big Bang, and Theories of Everything* (New York: Scientific American, 2015), 3.

45. Carlo Rovelli, "Now Means Nothing: How Time Works in Our Universe," *Discover*, May 31, 2018, https://www.discovermagazine.com/the-sciences/now-means-nothing-how-time-works-in-our-universe.

46. John Wheeler, cited in Musser, *Spooky*, 170.

47. Cited in Daniel J. Hughes, ed., *Moltke on the Art of War: Selected Writings* (New York: Presidio Press, 1993), 45–47.

48. Mike Berardino, "Mike Tyson explains one of his most famous quotes," *South Florida Sun-Sentinel*, November 9, 2012, https://www.sun-sentinel.com/sports/fl-xpm-2012-11-09-sfl-mike-tyson-explains-one-of-his-most-famous-quotes-20121109-story.html.

49. Mark 8:23–25.

50. Mark 2:12 (New English Bible).

51. Mark 6:2 (Wuest Expanded Translation).

52. Mark 3:21.

53. Mark 4:41.

54. Mark 6:51.

55. Mark 6:51 (New Revised Standard Version).

56. Mark 6:51 (Wuest Expanded Translation).

57. Mark 7:18.

58. John Smith, "The True Way or Method of Attaining Divine Knowledge," in Williams, *Select Discourses*, 3.

59. Susanna Wesley, cited in William Rainey Harper, Ernest DeWitt Burton, and Shailer Mathews, eds., *The Biblical World* (Chicago: University of Chicago Press, 1897), 10:452.

60. Mother Teresa, "On Prayer," in *Mystics, Visionaries, and Prophets: A Historical Anthology of Women's Spiritual Writings*, ed. Shawn Madigan (Minneapolis: Fortress Press, 1997), 421.

61. Lisa Feldman Barrett, *Seven and a Half Lessons About the Brain* (Boston: Houghton Mifflin, 2020), 87.

62. In the myth Aristophanes recounts in Plato's *Symposium*, all humans were originally part of a binary being and spend their lives in search of that primeval wholeness.

63. "History, 1838–1856, volume C-1 Addenda," *The Joseph Smith Papers*, 20, https://www.josephsmithpapers.org/paper-summary/history-1838-1856-volume-c-1-addenda/20.

64. Dorothy Dunnett, *Queens' Play* (New York: Vintage, 2019), 499.

65. Graham Greene, *The Power and the Glory* (New York: Penguin, 1990), 66.

66. Wolterstorff, *Lament for a Son*, 89.

67. Irenaeus, preface to "Irenaeus Against Heresies" III, in *ANF* 1:414.

68. Matt Ridley, *The Rational Optimist: How Prosperity Evolves* (New York: HarperCollins, 2010), 96.

69. John Meyendorff, *Byzantine Theology: Historical Trends and Doctrinal Themes* (New York: Fordham University Press, 1999), 143, 145.

70. I credit Nathaniel Givens with these insights; see his "Some Thoughts on Sin," *Times and Seasons*, July 29, 2013, https://www.timesand seasons.org/harchive/2013/07/some-thoughts-on-sin/.

71. Charles Taylor, *Secular Age* (Cambridge, MA: Harvard University Press, 2007), 655.

72. Sayers, *Mind of the Maker*, 110.

73. Rom. 5:11 in *Wycliffe Bible* (Cranbrook, British Columbia: Praotes, 2009), 748.

74. William Tyndale, in "Appendix 1," *Early Modern Communi(cati)ons: Studies in Early Modern English and Culture*, ed. Kinga Földváry and Erzsébet Stróbl (Newcastle, UK: Cambridge Scholars Publishing, 2012), 304.

75. Julian of Norwich, *Showings* VIII.18 (New York: Norton, 2005), 30. I have modernized some wording and spelling.

76. See Jacob's use in 2 Ne. 10:24 and Jacob 4:11 and Nephi's in 2 Ne. 25:23, 2 Ne. 33:9.

77. Julian of Norwich, *Showings* XIII.28, 41.

78. Luke 7:37.

79. Mark 10:52; Matt. 9:22; Luke 7:50.

80. Luke 7:50 (Amplified Bible).

81. Alma 7:12.

CHAPTER 4

1. Robert Burns, "To a Mouse," in *Poems: Chiefly in the Scottish Dialect* (Edinburgh: Luath Press, 2009), 121.

2. Morm. 5:2.

3. Rom. 5:2.

4. Col. 1:23.

5. 1 Thess. 1:3.

6. Paraphrased and cited in Alister McGrath, *Heresy: A History of Defending the Truth* (New York: HarperOne, 2009), 18.

7. Rom. 8:19, J. B. Phillips Version.

8. Clyde S. Kilby, *The Arts and the Christian Imagination: Essays on Art, Literature, and Aesthetics* (Brewster, MA: Paraclete Press, 2016), xvi.

9. Julian of Norwich, *Showings* XIII.40, 55. My rendering of the original.

10. Emanuel Swedenborg, *Heaven and Its Wonders and Hell* (West Chester, PA: Swedenborg Foundation, 1995), 73–74.

11. C. S. Lewis, *Till We Have Faces: A Myth Retold* (Boston: Houghton Mifflin, 2012), 294.

12. Francine R. Bennion, "A Latter-day Saint Theology of Suffering," in Jennifer Reeder and Kate Holbrook, eds., *At the Pulpit: 185 Years of Discourses by Latter-day Saint Women* (Salt Lake City, UT: Church Historian's Press, 2017), 224.

13. Jacob 4:14.

14. D&C 7:8.

15. In the Catholic soteriology, assurance of salvation comes, as Adolf von Harnack long ago stated, "by the doctrinal authority of the Church on the one side and by the Sacramental Church institution on the other." Adolf von Harnack, *History of Dogma*, trans. William M'Gilchrist (London: Williams & Norgate, 1899), 6:133. See my discussion of the quest for assurance in Terryl Givens, *Feeding the Flock: The Foundations of Mormon Thought: Church and Praxis* (New York: Oxford University Press, 2017).

16. Rev. 21:4.

17. Julian of Norwich, *Showings* XIV.51, 70–71.

18. Origen, "First Principles," II.xi.6, in *ANF* 4:299.

19. John 17:24, International Standard Version.

20. Kenneth Kirk, *The Vision of God: The Christian Doctrine of the Summum Bonum* (New York: Harper, 1966), 12–14.

21. Siphra on Leviticus 26:12, in Kirk, *Vision of God*, 22.

22. Luke 12:37.

23 George Herbert, "Love (3)," in *The Temple and Other English Poems* (London: Suttaby, 1883), 190.

24. Julian of Norwich, *Showings* VI.14, 21.

25. Joseph Smith, "History, 1838–1856, volume D-1 [1 August 1842–1 July 1843]," *The Joseph Smith Papers*, 4 [addenda], https://www.josephsmithpapers.org/paper-summary/history-1838-1856-volume-d-1-1-august-1842-1-july-1843/285.

26. As one scholar of Greek notes, "The passage (the Sermon on the Mount) contains plenty of imperatives (not jussive futures), where imperatives are wanted (e.g., at 5.44 ἀγαπᾶτε, προσεύχεσθε, ποιεῖτε) and plenty of future indicatives that are quite clearly to be understood as future indicatives and not as jussives. Note, too, that at 5.44 the present imperative ἀγαπᾶτε *replaces* the jussive future of the direct quote! Clearly Jesus himself prefers imperatives when he wants to issue a direct order." Julie Laskaris, personal communication with author, November 4, 2019.

27. Kenneth Wuest, *The New Testament: An Expanded Translation* (Grand Rapids, MI: Eerdmans, 1994).

28. Matt. 5:28 (Amplified Bible).

29. Julian of Norwich, *Showings* XIII.27, 39.

30. John Williams, *Stoner* (New York: Vintage, 2012), 201.

31. David Whyte, *What to Remember When Waking* (Audiobook, Sounds True, 2010).

32. Agnes Callard, *Aspiration* (New York: Oxford University Press, 2018), 172.

33. Callard, *Aspiration*, 231.

34. Hugh Nibley to President Ernest L. Wilkinson, February 22, 1952. Photocopy courtesy of Kristian Heal.

35. Irenaeus, "Against Heresies" III.xxiii.6, in *ANF* 1:457.

36. Baptism candidates were required "to fast one or two days before" the ordinance. "Teachings of the Twelve Apostles" VII, in *ANF* 7:379.

37. International Theological Commission, "The Hope of Salvation for Infants Who Die Without Being Baptized," 1.7.41, https://www.vatican.va/roman_curia/congregations/cfaith/cti_document/rc_con_cfaith_doc_20070419_un-baptised-infants_en.html.

38. Clement of Alexandria, "Exhortation to the Heathen 1," in *ANF* 2:174.

39. Clement of Alexandria, "Stromata" vii.x, in *ANF* 2:539.

40. Saint Basil the Great, "On the Spirit" ix.xxiii, in *NPNF2* 8:16; Gregory Nazianzen believed that, through the incarnation, Christ would "make me God." "Fourth Theological Oration [Oration 30]," in *NPNF2* 7:315.

41. James R. Payton Jr., "Keeping the End in View: How the Strange Yet Familiar Doctrine of Theosis Can Reinvigorate the Christian Life," *Christianity Today*, October 27, 2008, https://www.christianitytoday.com/ct/2008/october/theosis-deification-keeping-end-in-view.html.

42. *De Principiis* II.xi.6–7 paraphrased in Tripolitis, *Doctrine of the Soul*, 133.

43. William S. Harwell, ed., *Manuscript History of Brigham Young 1847–1850* (Salt Lake City, UT: Coller's, 1997), 156.

44. "Recognitions of Clement" I.lii, in *ANF* 8:91.

45. Rob Bell, *Love Wins: A Book about Heaven, Hell, and the Fate of Every Person Who Ever Lived* (New York: HarperOne, 2011), 6.

46. Origen, *Homilies 1–14*, 93.

47. Marcel Sarot, *God, Passibility, and Corporeality* (Kampen, Netherlands: Kok Pharos, 1992), 244.

48. Stephen H. Webb, *Jesus Christ, Eternal God: Heavenly Flesh and the Metaphysics of Matter* (New York: Oxford University Press, 2012), 249.

49. Christoph Markschies, *God's Body: Jewish, Christian, and Pagan Images of God* (Waco, TX: Baylor University Press, 2019), 324.

50. Marcus von Wellnitz, "The Catholic Liturgy and the Mormon Temple," *BYU Studies* 21, no. 1 (1981): 5.

51. S. G. F. Brandon, *The Fall of Jerusalem and the Christian Church* (London: SPCK, 1951), 120–21. This is not to say that early Christian worship in the Jerusalem temple would look like contemporary Latter-day Saint temple worship.

52. Cited in B. R. Rees, "Life," 132, in *Pelagius: Life and Letters* (Woodbridge, UK: Boydell Press, 1991).

53. Rees, *Pelagius*, "Letters," 10 in *Pelagius: Life and Letters*.

54. Elizabeth A. Clark, *The Origenist Controversy: The Cultural Construction of an Early Christian Debate* (Princeton, NJ: Princeton University Press, 1992), 245.

NOTES

55. 2 Ne. 26:24.

56. Kirk, *Vision of God*, 343–44.

57. Clement, *The Stromata* (London: Aeterna Press, 2016), vi, 638.

58. Joseph F. Smith, "Funeral Sermon," in *JD*, 19:264.

59. John 3:17. I have rendered the Greek *sozo* as "heal" rather than the KJV "save."

60. Thomas Traherne, *Centuries of Meditations*, in *The Works of Thomas Traherne*, ed. Jan Ross (Cambridge: D. S. Drewer, 2013), 12.

61. 1 Cor. 11:32 (Modern Literal Version).

62. Dieter F. Uchtdorf, "O How Great the Plan of Our God!," *Ensign* 46, no. 11 (November 2016): 21.

63. James E. Talmage, "Conference Report" (Salt Lake City, UT: The Church of Jesus Christ of Latter-day Saints, April 1930), 97.

64. Gerard Manley Hopkins, *Poems of Gerard Manley Hopkins: Now First Published*, ed. Robert Bridges (n.p.: Pantianos Classics, 1918), poem 54.

65. Arthur Schopenhauer, *Studies in Pessimism: A Series of Essays* (London: Swan Sonnenschein, 1891), 69.

66. John 10:10.

67. Robinson Jeffers, *The Wild God of the World: An Anthology of Robinson Jeffers*, ed. Albert Gelpi (Stanford: Stanford University Press, 2003), 23.

68. Francis Darwin, ed., *The Life and Letters of Charles Darwin* (London: John Murray, 1887), 43.

EPILOGUE

1. Gilbert K. Chesterton, *Orthodoxy* (New York: Dover, 2004), 12.

2. Parley P. Pratt, *The World Turned Upside Down* (Liverpool, UK: James and Woodburn, 1842), 18–19.

3. Ehat and Cook, *Words of Joseph Smith*, 238, 244, 246, 256.

4. Matthew Stewart, *The Courtier and the Heretic: Leibniz, Spinoza, and the Fate of God in the Modern World* (New York: Norton, 2006), 38.

5. Virginia Sorensen, *A Little Lower than the Angels* (New York: Knopf, 1942; Salt Lake City, UT: Signature Books, 1998), 55.

6. William Shakespeare, *Hamlet*, 1.5.167–68.

7. George MacDonald, *Thomas Wingfold, Curate* (London: Hurst and Blackett, 1876), 3:65–66.

Scripture Index

OLD TESTAMENT

NEW TESTAMENT

BOOK OF MORMON

Scripture Index

INDEX

INDEX